B

Antediluvian. Cavil. Discomfit. Encomium. Ineluctable. Ne plus ultra. Peripatetic. Physiognomy. Saturnine. Solipsism. Torpor.

If you're like most of us, when you last read or heard these words, you didn't know what they meant.

The Words You Should Know features definitions and sample sentences for over 1200 tough-but-common words that every educated person should be able to use and define.

THE WORDS YOU SHOULD KNOW

DAVID OLSEN

THE WORDS YOU SHOULD KNOW

DAVID OLSEN

1200 essential words every educated person should be able to use and define.

Adams Media Corporation
AVON, MASSACHUSETTS

Published by Adams Media, an F+W Publications Company
57 Littlefield Street, Avon, MA 02322. U.S.A.
www.adamsmedia.com

ISBN: 1-55850-018-9

Printed in Canada.

Z Y X W

This publication is designed to provide accurate and authoritative information with regard to the subject matter covered. It is sold with the understanding that the publisher is not engaged in rendering legal, accounting, or
other professional advice. If legal advice or other expert assistance is
required, the services of a competent professional person should be sought.
— From a *Declaration of Principles* jointly adopted by a Committee of the
American Bar Association and a Committee of Publishers and Associations

Special thanks are due to Elizabeth Gale for her help.

This book is available at quantity discounts for bulk purchases.
For information, call 1-800-872-5627.

Table of Contents

About This Book

One of the main advantages of *The Words You Should Know* is what it does not contain.

Reading the dictionary is virtually no one's idea of a thrilling time. Accordingly, this book has been designed to be that rarity among vocabulary books: one you can leaf through enjoyably. You will not find here long chunks of dense type examining the thirty-one different potential uses of the word *make*. The focus here is on the most popularly employed senses of tough-but-common words. Where a word is in common usage in more than one main mode--as both a noun and a verb, for instance--both of the common definitions are included. No attempt is made here to render every conceivable usage of every word included in the book. That would be boring. The objective of *The Words You Should Know* is simply to help you become familiar with the most common senses of the difficult words you are likely to encounter.

D.O.

abash *(uh-BASH)*, *verb*
To disconcert, humiliate, or shame. To *abash* is to make another feel uncomfortable or disconcerted, or to cause someone to lose composure.

> *The older boys had no qualms about abashing the new arrivals; it was an old tradition at the school.*

abate *(uh-BATE)*, *verb*
To put an end to or reduce in intensity. To *abate* is to reduce or diminish something. Something that lessens or weakens is abating.

> *The flood waters abated when the rain stopped.*

abdicate *(AB-di-kate)*, *verb*
To formally give up a position or responsibility. To *abdicate* means to step down from a high government office or other powerful position. Originally, the word referred primarily to royalty.

> *The King, as we all know, abdicated rather than give up the woman he loved.*

aberration *(ab-uh-RAY-shun)*, *noun*
Diverging from a moral standard or expected course. *Aberration* refers to a usually temporary departure from what is normal or expected. Something that deviates from a customary or natural course of action is an *aberration*.

> *Sally's poor work in the first part of October was hardly grounds for dismissal; it was an aberration caused by serious problems at home.*

abet *(uh-BET)*, *verb*
To encourage or assist a plan or activity. To *abet* is to

entice or help, usually in a misdeed. An accomplice to a robbery *abets* the crime.

> *Though Michael did not participate in the actual kidnapping, he left himself open to charges of abetting the perpetrators by hiding them from the police.*

abhorrent *(ab-HOR-ent), adjective*
Loathsome or contemptible. *Abhorrent* refers to something that is is reprehensible or repulsive. That which is repugnant or detestable is *abhorrent*.

> *Julie found the book's recounting of the details of serial murders particularly abhorrent.*

abide *(Uh-BIDE), verb*
To withstand, patiently wait for, or tolerate. To *abide* is to tolerate or endure. *Abiding* also refers to the ability to withstand and/or persevere.

> *I could abide my dinner companion's bigotry for only so long; by evening's end, I had to challenge him.*

abject *(AB-jekt), adjective*
Utter hopelessness, destitution, or resignation. *Abject* refers to the worst or most miserable kind of something. Anything disheartening and hopelessly low is *abject*.

> *It is high time we did something about the abject suffering of the impoverished in that war-torn nation.*

abjure *(ab-JOOR), verb*
To renounce, repudiate, or reject one's word or professed beliefs. To *abjure* is to solemnly swear off or recant.

After some soul-searching following his financial and domestic problems, Brad abjured drinking and gambling.

ablution *(ah-BLOO-shun), noun*
Washing or cleansing the body as part of a religious rite; any cleansing, purification, or purging. *Ablution* is the washing away or cleansing of sin or spiritual uncleanness.

Pilate turned away from the crowd and called for a bowl of scented water with which to perform his ablutions.

abnegate *(AB-ne-gate), verb*
To renounce, surrender, or deny privilege to oneself. *Abnegation* is the act of denying oneself something considered vital or important. Hunger strikes or long fasts are a form of *abnegation*.

The activist's fast lasted for 47 days; in an election year, such abnegation draws headlines and attention from elected officials.

aboriginal *(ab-uh-RIDGE-ih-nul), adjective*
Indigenous or native to an area; the first of its kind in a region. *Aboriginal* pertains most commonly to the aborigines in Australia. However, the most complete definition of the word is something that existed first in an area. The aborigines in Australia were that area's first inhabitants.

The General Assembly was presented with a petition on environmental matters signed by representatives of the world's various aboriginal peoples.

abortive *(uh-BOR-tive), adjective*
Unsuccessful or fruitless. Something that is *abortive* has failed to come to fruition. The word also refers to something that is partially or imperfectly developed.

> *Although it was the astronauts' failure to dock at the station that drew media attention, the abortive mission had many potentially more serious problems as well.*

abrade *(uh-BRADE), verb*
To wear away or rub off; to wear down in spirit. To *abrade* is to erode or break down. Sandpaper *abrades* the surface of wood.

> *The campaign had hoped for a hard-hitting, informative television commercial, but the ad--widely perceived as negative and mean-spirited--served only to abrade voter support.*

abrogate *(AB-ro-gate), verb*
To nullify or cancel. *Abrogation* is an official action used to formally and unilaterally conclude an agreement or deed. Something that has been repealed or abolished has been abrogated.

> *The United States abrogated the treaty after evidence appeared suggesting that the other nations had failed to honor the agreement.*

abscond *(ab-SKOND), verb*
To depart quickly and in secret, especially to avoid criminal charges. To *abscond* is to secretly flee the consequences of one's acts, particularly those acts leading to illicit gain. Prosecuting attorneys might accuse someone convicted of embezzling of absconding with company funds if the person left the firm shortly after the alleged crime.

The bank robbers immediately absconded with the money to Mexico.

absolve *(ab-ZOLV), verb*
To formally pronounce guiltless or blameless. To *absolve* is to relieve of any responsibility for an actual or alleged misdeed. In the legal sense, absolution carries with it implication that the authorities no longer hold that the individual committed the misdeed.
The judge absolved the accused of any wrongdoing.

abstemious *(ab-STEE-me-us), adjective*
Consuming food and drink in moderation. Those who are *abstemious* restrict themselves to the bare necessities of life. In a larger sense, the word can refer to any austere or unassuming lifestyle.

Despite the hardships of his abstemious way of life, the monk radiated the confidence that comes with knowing one has chosen the correct path.

abstinence *(AB-ste-nence), noun*
Voluntarily foregoing the indulgence of an appetite. *Abstinence* is the act of abstaining from food, drink, or pleasure. *Abstinence* may refer to denial of certain foods and drinks thought to be harmful to one's health; however, it can also refer to refraining from behavior considered immoral.

After years of indulgence, it was difficult for Evelyn to follow her doctor's order of complete abstinence from liquor.

abstruse *(ab-STROOCE), adjective*
Complex and difficult to comprehend. *Abstruse* refers to

something complex or specialized that requires special effort to grasp.

Scientists may understand Einstein's theory of relativity, but for most laymen it remains an abstruse collection of surrealistic ideas.

a capella *(ah kuh-PELL-a), (Music)*

Singing without musical accompaniment. Used as an adjective, *a capella* often refers to a rhythmic and highly inventive vocal style.

The group's a capella rendition of "The Star Spangled Banner" was remarkably good, especially considering that the song is quite difficult to sing with musical accompaniment.

accede *(ak-SEED), verb*

To give one's consent. To *accede* is to signal one's acceptance of something. To formally accept a high position is to *accede*. Therefore, someone who accepts a position *accedes* to that office.

The college president eventually acceded to the demands of the student demonstrators.

accentuate *(ak-SEN-choo-ate), verb*

To intensify or accent. To *accentuate* something is to emphasize or stress it. To strengthen or heighten the effect of something is to *accentuate* it.

Brian's new glasses accentuate his nose unflatteringly.

accolade *(AK-uh-lade), noun*

A mark of acknowledgment or expression of praise.

Originally, an *accolade* was the ceremonial bestowal of knighthood upon a person, with a sword tapped on each shoulder. That which confers praise or honor is an *accolade*.

> *The firm's president had hung on his office wall many plaques, citations, and accolades.*

accord *(uh-CORD)*, *noun*
A formal reaching of agreement. An *accord* is reached when a settlement or compromise of conflicting views occurs.

> *After a prolonged strike, with the issue of healthcare benefits was resolved, the representatives finally reached an accord acceptable to both labor and management.*

accrue *(uh-CRUE)*, *verb*
To accumulate or grow. To *accrue* can mean the act of something's increasing or accumulating by gradual means. Money held in a bank will accumulate (or *accrue*) interest.

> *She disputed the bank's figures on the interest her account had accrued.*

acculturation *(uh-kul-chu-RAY-shun)*, *noun*
Alteration of one culture traceable to interaction with another. *Acculturation* describes the process of cultural influences as well as the means by which the culture of a particular culture is instilled in a human being.

> *While there are often severe adjustment problems among senior citizens who immigrate to this country, acculturation among younger children occurs remarkably quickly.*

acquiescence *(ak-wee-ESS-unce)*, *noun*
The act of passive agreement or assent without objection. *Acquiesence* is the act of assenting or complying with another's demands. Someone who submits to another's will is acquiescent.

> *Hank, enchanted by first-time grandfatherhood, gave over to complete acquiescence on his first day with little Laura.*

acrid *(AK-rid)*, *adjective*
Biting or harsh in odor or taste; deeply or violently bitter. *Acrid* refers to anything unpleasantly sharp and pungent to the senses of smell or taste. *Acrid* can also be used to describe a bitter or harsh verbal exchange between persons.

> *Florence's acrid remarks did not sit well with the Board of Directors.*

acrimonious *(ak-ri-MO-nee-us)*, *adjective*
Mean-spirited, bitter, or ill-natured. *Acrimonious* refers to language or exchanges that are filled with animosity. Something characterized by sharpness or bitterness of speech is acrimonious.

> *Divorce is, we must remember, an expensive, emotionally devastating, and acrimonious affair.*

acrophobia *(ak-ruh-FO-bee-a)*, *noun*
An abnormal fear of heights. *Acrophobia* refer s to person's fear of high places; it is characterized by fealings of dread, danger, and helplessness.

> *Of course, his acrophobia ruled out any ride in the hot-air bolloon.*

acumen *(uh-CUE-men), noun*
Keenness of judgment. *Acumen* refers to an ability to make quick, accurate decisions and evaluations. It is characterized by rapid discernment and insight.

> *After only two years as a restaurant owner, Clyde developed a remarkable business acumen; in a supposedly "bad location," he had little trouble coming up with promotions that attracted customers.*

acute *(uh-CUTE), adjective*
Sharp, shrewd, or severe. *Acute* can refer to something that is severe or sharp (for instance, an *acute* pain). It can also means "marked by keen discernment or intellectual perception."

> *After she fell off the horse, Doris felt an acute pain in her side.*

adage *(AD-ij), noun*
A short proverb or saying. An *adage* is a brief maxim. "A stitch in time saves nine" is an example of an *adage*.

> *The old man quoted adages endlessly, which the reporter dutifully took down in his notebook.*

adamant *(AD-uh-munt), adjective*
Unwilling to submit; stubborn and unyielding. Historically, *adamant* refers to a legendary stone of infinite hardness. (The word *diamond* shares the same root.)

> *Despite the objections of their families, Robin and Tim were adamant about moving away from the town in which they had been raised.*

addendum *(uh-DEN-dum)*, *noun*

Something additional; an item to be added on. An *addendum* is something that is added (for instance, a supplement to a book),.

Before we adjourn, please let me add the following brief addendum to the record.

adduce *(uh-DUCE)*, *verb*

To cite as an example or justification. To *adduce* is to bring something forward for consideration. To cite an example or put forth a proposition is to *adduce*.

I would adduce the following reasons in support of rewriting the club charter.

adept *(uh-DEPT)*, *adjective*

Proficient; expert; highly skilled. *Adept* refers to someone who is very good at performing a given task.

Hans, an adept formulator of crossword puzzles, sometimes seems to me to have memorized the entire dictionary.

adherent *(ad-HERE-unt)*, *noun*

Someone who adheres to an opinion. *Adherent* describes one who is devoted to or strongly associated with a cause or opinion.

The measure's adherents were outspent by its opponents.

ad hoc *(ad HOK)*, *adjective*

For a specific purpose or end; formed for immediate or

present need. This Latin phrase translates literally to "for this purpose." Anything that is designed or set aside for a specific purpose may be referred to as *ad hoc*.

> *The council established an ad hoc committee to review textbook standards in face of the sudden complaints from parents.*

ad infinitum *(ad in-fi-NEYE-tum), adjective*
Without end. Literally, "to infinity." The phrase refers to things without end or to something that is limitless. In practical use, *ad infinitum* usually carries a sense of ironic overstatement.

> *Wilbur remarked wryly that he could probably discuss the treatment facility's weaknesses ad infinitum.*

adjudicate *(ad-JOO-di-cate), verb*
To employ judicial procedure as a means of hearing and settling a case. To *adjudicate* is to have a judge or someone in authority reach a decision on some difficult point. It is usually reserved to describe processes of resolution within a legal setting.

> *Gentlemen, if this case is hard for you to argue, rest assured it is equally difficult for me to adjudicate.*

adjure (ad-JOOR), verb
To command solemnly as if under oath. To *adjure* is to command or enjoin solemnly, often under the threat of some sort of penalty.

> *The witnesses were adjured to avoid any contact with the accused.*

adroit *(uh-DROIT), adjective*
Nimble, expert, or skillful in the use of one's hands or body; adept at accomplishing one's aim. A person who is deft or expert at a task, or who shows uncommon ingenuity or skill, is said to be *adroit*.

> *Matthew, an adroit swordsman, easily bested his opponent.*

adulation *(ad-yoo-LAY-shun), noun*
Extreme praise, admiration, or flattery, especially of a servile nature. *Adulation* is generally taken to describe acclaim and admiration that is out of scope with its object.

> *Despite great hardship, upheaval, and death resulting from the violent tactics of the secret police, adulation of Stalin continued as though the country was paradise itself.*

adulterate *(a-DUL-ter-ate), verb*
To make impure or tainted. To *adulterate* is to reduce the quality of something--for instance, by substituting inferior ingredients. An unadulterated product is one that retains its original high quality and has not been tampered with in any way.

> *At the turn of the century, the sale of adulterated dairy products in the U.S.* caused a major scandal.

aesthetic *(us-THET-ik), adjective*
Of or related to a sense of what is attractive or beautiful. Also: Related to sensation and feeling as contrasted with reason or logic. *Aesthetics* is the science that examines how people react to art and to beauty. Something that is aesthetically pleasing is in keeping with one's standards of scale, structure, clarity, and attractiveness.

It is not my place to comment on the aesthetics of the car; I am here to report on whether it won the race, which it did.

affect *(uh-FEKT), verb*
To influence or produce an effect on. *Affect* is often confused with *effect*, which (as a verb) means "to bring about or accomplish (a thing)." (See *effect*.) In addition, to *affect* (an emotion or style, for instance) is to pretend to have, be, or feel.

Jane's affectations have really begun to bother me, and I think they have started to affect her relationships with other people as well.

affinity *(uh-FIN-ih-tee), noun*
A natural attraction or inherent similarity between two things. To have an *affinity* for something is to like it almost by instinct, without any effort or thought. Similarly, ideas or concepts that are related in basic ways or have close connections are said to have *affinity*.

My affinity for the works of Poe is well documented in previous letters to you.

affirmative *(uh-FIR-muh-tive), adjective*
Positive in nature; factually valid. *Affirmative* is the opposite of negative; its use means the subject has vouched for and affirmed the correctness of a statement or idea.

When asked whether or not he lived at 1267 Main, the defendant answered in the affirmative.

affliction *(uh-FLICK-shun), noun*
Suffering; a state of pain. An *affliction* is a state of misery or disabling disease.

Carl's arthritis was at times quite painful, but he found the most remarkable ways to work around his affliction.

agape *(ah-GAH-pay), noun*

In Christianity, divine love for humanity, or human love that transcends customary boundaries. *Agape* is the Greek word for love. Today, it is often used to describe an unselfish love that goes beyond sexuality or other worldly concerns.

> *The nurse's work among the poor and dispossessed seemed rooted, not in a well-meaning and temporary humanitarian instinct, but in a deeper and more profound agape totally unfamiliar to most of us.*

aggrandize *(uh-GRAND-ize), verb*

To raise the importance of or make to appear great. To *aggrandize* is to increase the prestige, influence, reputation, or power of a person or institution.

> *What had started out as a simple report quickly degenerated into meaningless self-promotion; Peter could not resist the urge to aggrandize himself.*

agnosticism *(ag-NOS-ti-sihz-um), noun*

The belief that it is impossible to know whether or not an ultimate cause (that is, God). exists. An *agnostic* is a person who is unable to conclude that there is or is not a God. By contrast, an atheist is a person who has concluded that God does not exist. (The two words are often confused.).

> *Frank, who had been raised in a deeply religious home, knew that it would hurt his parents to speak openly of his agnosticism.*

akin *(uh-KIN), adjective*
Showing a similar feature or quality. Two things that are comparable or related in some important way are said to be *akin*.

> *I feel that Harry's repeated falsification of his records is much more than a breach of policy: it is akin to outright perjury.*

alacrity *(uh-LACK-rih-tee), noun*
Eager, cheerful rapidity or promptness. Someone who is willing to extend themselves politely and quickly for another is said to show *alacrity*.

> *Jones made a special effort to show alacrity his first day on the job.*

albatross *(AL-buh-tross), noun*
A significant impediment, handicap, or burden. Also: a large pelican-like bird. The most common idiomatic use of *albatross* is the first sense given above.

> *In Coleridge's poem* The Rime of the Ancient Mariner, *a sailor shoots a friendly albatross and is made to wear the bird's carcass around his neck.*

allay *(uh-LAY), verb*
To ease or put something (for instance, a doubt or concern), to rest; to mitigate; to calm or quiet by placing matters in perspective. A person who points out the unjustified basis of a fear is said to *allay* the fear.

> *I know there have been rumors that the project will be quite expensive, but I think you will agree that these figures allay that fear.*

allude *(uh-LOOD), verb*
To make passing reference to. A person who gives a few
details but does not describe an event openly and
completely could be said to *allude* to that event. Similarly,
someone who makes a brief reference to an incident in a
certain novel is considered to have made an allusion to
the work.

> *I am aware of the incident you are alluding to, Mr.*
> *Mayor, but I am afraid you have been misinformed*
> *about the events of that night.*

altruism *(AL-troo-ihz-um), noun*
Selflessness; good-natured action intended for the
betterment of others. *Altruism* is the quality of acting in
the aid of another (often a previously unknown person or
group of unknown persons) without any self-interest or
promise of reward. A person who offers shelter to a
dispossessed stranger could be said to show *altruism*.

> *For six years Vernon--an outwardly cold man--had*
> *worked tirelessly at the shelter, but his coworkers*
> *suspected nothing of his altruism.*

amalgamate *(uh-MAL-guh-mate), verb*
To blend into a coherent single unit. Originally, an
amalgamation was the mixture of an alloy or metal with
mercury. Today, to *amalgamate* is taken to mean to
combine of a number of elements into a whole.

> *The two boards voted to amalgamate the firms as*
> *soon as possible.*

ambience *(AWM-bee-awnce), noun*

A feeling or atmosphere associated with a place or individual. The distinctive air patrons may associate with a certain restaurant, for instance, can be a large part of its appeal; this atmospheric "feel" is called *ambience*.

> *The old mansion had the ambience of an elegant, refined gentleman unaccustomed to being hurried.*

ambidextrous *(am-bih-DEX-truss), adjective*

Capable of using both hands with equal skill. *Ambidextrous* is made up of two halves from old Latin words: "ambi-", meaning both, and "dexter", meaning right. The idea is that an ambidextrous person is able to act as though he has "two right hands."

> *Since the juggler was ambidextrous, she could start her routine with a circular motion to either the left or the right.*

ambiguous *(am-BIG-yoo-us), adjective*

Unclear; capable of supporting a number of differing interpretations. *Ambiguous* can refer to a person as well as a passage in a piece of writing.

> *It was clear from his note that he had left the country, but on the matter of his final destination the writer was ambiguous.*

ambivalent *(am-BIV-uh-lent), adjective*

Of two minds; uncertain as to which position or course of action to take. Someone who has feelings or thoughts that are in conflict with each other is said to be *ambivalent*.

> *Frank had been ambivalent about marriage in his early years; now, at thirty-five, he was eager to settle down.*

amble *(AM-bul), verb*
To walk in an easy or leisurely manner; to saunter or stroll. To *amble* is to go at an unhurried pace. Someone who explores a garden by walking through it slowly and reflectively at a comfortable pace could be said to *amble* through the garden.

> *The day's last customer ambled from one end of the shop to the other; no amount of staring from the clerk, it seemed, could make him come to the register.*

ameliorate *(uh-MEEL-yuh-rate), verb*
To improve or upgrade. To *ameliorate* is to make better or put right. When an unacceptable state of affairs is changed for the better, it can be said to have been *ameliorated*.

> *The ambassador's midnight visit was the first step toward ameliorating the poor relations between the two countries, and may actually have averted war.*

amenable *(uh-MEH-nuh-bul), adjective*
Agreeable (to an idea); open to suggestion or willing to heed advice. A person who yields to the suggestion or wishes of another is said to be *amenable* to the idea in question. The word carries a sense of tact and manageability rather than submissiveness.

> *We expected stiff opposition to the new benefits package, but once we took the trouble to explain it thoroughly the employees were quite amenable.*

amend *(uh-MEND), verb*
To formally alter from the original. Also: To rectify or improve upon. To *amend* something usually means to

repair or alter it in face of a new and/or unanticipated situation. When the United States Constitution is *amended*, for instance, specific new language is ratified to expand or clarify the document.

> *In light of the new proposal, I think it is appropriate to amend the remarks I made here yesterday.*

amenity *(un-MEN-ih-tee), noun*

A pleasant manner or custom. Also: A component or feature that gives pleasure or satisfaction. While the primary meaning of *amenity* has to do with the customs of social interaction, its use in advertising and sales settings to mean "a convenient and desirable extra" has gained ground in recent years.

> *Chris's home, which was once spare, now featured all the amenities: a microwave oven, a sauna, an entertainment center, and even a new swimming pool in the back.*

amiable *(AY-me-uh-bul), adjective*

Possessing a pleasant, cordial nature. A person who has a happy disposition and is easy to get along with is said to be *amiable*.

> *^SJeanne made it a point to speak to everyone at the party; she came across as quite an amiable hostess.*

amoral *(ay-MOR-uhl), adjective*

Without moral discretion or standards. To be *amoral* is to act as though the distinctions of right and wrong are nonexistent. A person who is amoral is neither moral nor immoral.

> *In the end, we find that war is not always "for the*

*right," nor even "evil," but far too often a
completely amoral exercise.*

amorous *(AM-er-us), adjective*
Strongly disposed toward love or sexuality. Someone who is
amorous is preoccupied with thoughts of love, especially
sexual love.

> *The young man's amorous attentions merely annoyed
> Rose.*

amorphous *(uh-MOR-fuss), adjective*
Formless. *Amorphous* refers not only to physical
shapelessness, but also to ideas, works of art or literature,
and even personalities that are vague or poorly defined.

> *He did not make reasoned arguments in defense of
> his client, but rather an amorphous collection of
> unsupported claims that persuaded no one.*

amortize *(AH-muhr-tize), verb*
To settle a debt by means of installment payments.   Also:
To write off an asset's value over a certain period.   To
amortize is to liquidate with periodic payments.

> *The debt will be completely amortized in two
> years.*

anachronism *(uh-NAK-ruh-niz-um), adjective*
The depiction of something as occurring or existing at a
point in time it did not. An *anachronism* is an intentional
or unintentional representation of a historically incorrect
situation. A portrait of George Washington holding a pocket
calculator would be an example of an *anachronism*.

> *The author's weak grasp of Greek history is*

demonstrated by several embarrassing anachronisms in the book's very first chapter.

analogous *(uh-NAL-uh-gus)*, *adjective*

Similar to such a degree that an analogy may be drawn. An analogy is a similarity or comparison between two items, ideas, or features; something is *analogous* to something else when it can be shown to share a significant corresponding element with it.

Historically, the American expansion westward to the Pacific is analogous to the Russian expansion eastward across Siberia.

anarchy *(AN-ar-key)*, *noun*

The absence of government; a disordered and uncontrolled situation. Originally, *anarchy* referred to a specific doctrine advocating voluntary associations among individuals and arguing against any empowered government or rule of law. Today, *anarchy* is generally used to describe a temporarily chaotic social situation in which no central authority exists.

After the death of the Queen, many in the council feared a return to the anarchy of a decade earlier.

anathema *(uh-NATH-eh-muh)*, *noun*

A person or thing regarded as wrong in the highest degree; a loathsome entity. To say something is *anathema* to a person is to say that it is as detestable and unacceptable to him as it can possibly be. The word has its root in a kind of formal religious curse or denunciation.

The ambassador warned us ahead of time not to attempt to discuss the issue of dropping sanctions against the dictator; that subject is anathema to his government.

ancillary *(AN-se-lare-ree)*, *adjective*

Secondary or subordinate; serving an auxiliary or supportive function. An *ancillary* role is a role that does not "command the spotlight," but that may entail support duties of some importance.

> *He took a great deal of pride in his work, even though the pay was poor and most of his duties were ancillary to those of the regional director.*

androgynous *(an-DROJ-uh-nuss)*, *adjective*

Showing characteristics reminiscent of both man and woman. This word does not refer to a supposed individual possessing both male and female reproductive organs; that would be a hermaphrodite. Someone who is *androgynous* has traits normally considered naturally male or female. (*Androgynous* may also refer to someone who shows no strong gender signs at all.)

> *The androgynous appearance of some young boys explains how Shakespeare could write a "woman's" part like Juliet and yet never see it performed by a woman.*

anecdote *(AN-ik-dote)*, *noun*

A short account of an interesting event. *Anecdote* is frequently confused with *antidote*, which means "a medical remedy."

> *The chairman's anecdotes are amusing, but they are hardly the stuff of leadership.*

anglicize *(ANG-gli-size)*, *verb*

To render into the forms of English or to make similar to English. To *anglicize* a word or name is to change it in a way that allows it to resemble other English words more closely. Many immigrants to this country anglicized family names (for instance, from Bodini to Bonney).

> *My grandfather came to this country in 1904 under the name of Mikhail Zarensky, which he anglicized to Michael Zare.*

animosity *(an-ih-MOSS-ih-tee), noun*
Intense hostility toward a person or thing, usually taking the form of action. *Animosity* is a bitter dislike directed at something or someone.

> *Clyde's first few months on the job were fine, but after he was transferred to a new department he came to harbor real animosity toward his supervisor.*

annunciate *(uh-NUN-see-ate), verb*
To proclaim or announce. *Annunciate* is a more formal, sometimes religiously oriented way to express the idea of proclaiming or announcing.

> *The annunciation of the Virgin Mary figures importantly in Catholicism.*

anomaly *(uh-NOM-a-lee), noun*
A seemingly abnormal example; a deviation from established form. When something differs markedly from the expected order of things, it is an *anomaly*.

> *Bill, who was raised in a family of avid golfers, is something of an anomaly: he thinks the sport is boring.*

antebellum *(an-teh-BELL-uhm), adjective*
Of or pertaining to the period preceding the American Civil War. *Antebellum* translates from the Latin as "before

the war."

> *Nostalgia aside, we should remember that for those held in slavery the antebellum period was anything but romantic and chivalrous.*

antecedent *(AN-tih-see-dent)*, *noun*
A trend, idea, fashion, historical event, etc., that came before. Also: An earlier word to which a pronoun refers. (In the sentence "The car was painted blue, though it had a huge red rust mark," *car* is the *antecedent* of *it*.)

> *Remember, writers: the antecedent always goes first in the sentence.*

antediluvian *(an-ti-de-LOO-vee-en)*, *adjective*
Pertaining to the period prior to the Great Flood recounted in the Bible. Figuratively, *antediluvian* has come to mean woefully out-of-date or extremely old-fashioned.

> *Rachel's ideas are outmoded, but those in Paul's report are practically antediluvian.*

antipathy *(an-TIP-uh-thea)*, *noun*
A feeling of strong revulsion or dislike. *Antipathy* is a combination of the Greek forms "anti" (against or in opposition to) and "pathos" (having to do with one's feelings and emotions). Therefore, *antipathy* is a feeling of aversion.

> *I'm afraid my antipathy for light opera won't be changed by a single night out.*

antiquity *(an-TIK-wi-tee)*, *noun*
The quality of pertaining to long ago or dating back to ancient times. *Antiquity* can be applied to anything old or

ancient, but it is often used to refer specifically to the Middle Ages.

> *The goblet's origin, we must now admit, is lost in the mists of antiquity.*

antithesis *(an-TITH-i-sis), noun*
The opposite or highest possible contrast. *Antithesis* refers to the exact opposite of a given thing. *Antithesis* is also the name of a form in rhetoric in which two ideas are contrasted dramatically: "We will live as heroes or die in the attempt."

> *Mr. Brown--haggard, unkempt, and exhausted--looked like the very antithesis of the charismatic achiever we'd heard about.*

aphorism *(AYF-ur-iz-um), noun*
A short saying that illustrates an important principle or observation. An *aphorism* is a concise summation of opinion or received wisdom, for example: "You never get a second chance to make a first impression."

> *Early American readers found Franklin's Poor Richard's Almanac to be a rich repository of wit, political commentary, forecasts, humor, aphorisms, and unapologetic gossip.*

aplomb *(ah-PLOM), noun*
Assurance. *Aplomb* refers to one's poise and self-confidence.

> *Although her debating opponent subjected her to many attacks, Jane handled them all with aplomb.*

apocalyptic *(uh-pok-uh-LIP-tik), adjective*
Having to do with revelation or prophecy. Also: presaging

imminent destruction or disaster. In part because the final book of the Bible, Revelation, outlines prophecies of the end of the world, *apocalypse* has come to suggest a cataclysmic conflict of forces, and *apocalyptic* to reflect a sense of imminent mass destruction.

> *The novel's apocalyptic ending may be appropriate, but it is still heartrendingly difficult to read of violence on this large a scale.*

apocryphal *(uh-POK-ri-fuhl), adjective*
Of dubious authenticity. A story that is fabricated long after the fact is considered *apocryphal*. (Similarly, several books of the Bible that are not universally accepted by all Christians form a body of work known as the Apocrypha.)

> *The story of Shakespeare's having shared a mistress with Richard Burbage is almost certainly apocryphal.*

apparition *(ap-uh-RISH-en), noun*
A spirit or ghost; a supernatural appearance. *Apparition* can also refer to anything that appears quickly and unexpectedly, as though by supernatural influence.

> *In dim light, the guests held hands around the table, half expecting to see an apparition at any moment.*

appelation *(ap-puh-LAY-shun), noun*
Title or name. An *appelation* is the formal name of something.

> *I wish you would stop calling me Doctor; I have never gone by that appelation.*

apprehension *(ap-ri-HEN-sun), noun*
Uneasiness about the future; suspicion of impending bad

fortune. Also: The act of arresting or stopping. Another sense of *apprehension* is "idea or understanding."

> *A vague feeling of apprehension came over Gordon as he stepped into the old house.*

apprise *(uh-PRISE), verb*
To supply notice to. *Apprising* someone of something means bringing them up to date or informing them of it.

> *After the president was apprised of the latest developments in the Middle East, he decided to postpone his speech to the nation.*

apropos *(ap-ruh-POE) adverb*
Opportunely; as an apt point. The structure is typically "*apropos* of . . . ", meaning "speaking of . . . " or "with regard to . . . ". The word comes from the French for "to the purpose of . . . ".

> *Apropos of our vacation, it occurs to me that we haven't yet selected a hotel in Honolulu.*

arbiter *(AR-bi-ter), noun*
A person selected to judge or mediate an issue in dispute. An *arbiter* is the person assigned to power to make a final decision. A person selected to rule definitively on a salary dispute, for example, would be an arbiter.

> *It is not my plan to ask an arbiter to step in; I firmly believe you and I can settle this amicably between ourselves.*

arbitrary *(AR-bih-trer-ee), adjective*
Unregulated by law or reason; determined by impulse. *Arbitrary* refers to decisions made, not according to

established procedures or laws, but purely through the discretion of an individual. It carries a sense of capriciousness or even lack of responsibility.

> *The rules you have laid down for this contest are completely arbitrary and have no basis in past tournaments.*

ardent *(AR-dent), adjective*
Intense, passionate, devoted; characterized by high emotion. *Ardent* people show great enthusiasm for causes and people close to them.

> *Barbara, an ardent stamp collector, has the most impressive collection of French stamps in the school.*

arduous *(AR-joo-us), adjective*
Requiring exceptional effort or care. Something is *arduous* if it is mentally or physically challenging, or if it pushes one to the limit of one's abilities.

> *Stacy has been preparing all week for the arduous marathon competition.*

aromatic *(air-o-MAT-ik), adjective*
Possessing a pleasant odor. An *aromatic* flower is one that is pleasing to the smell. Many sweet-scented things share a certain chemical structure known as an *aromatic compound.*

> *The herbs lent what would have been an ordinary meal a satisfying aromatic touch.*

ascetic *(uh-SET-ik), noun*
A person who chooses a life of constant and strict self-denial, usually as an act of faith. An *ascetic* is someone

who foregoes the conveniences of society in order to lead a life of self-discipline and contemplation. *Asceticism* is the body of beliefs and philosophies by which ascetics live their lives.

> *At first Michael had doubts about his religious calling, but he eventually discovered that his tendency toward solitude and introspection were well suited to the life of an ascetic.*

ascribe *(uh-SKRYBE)*, *verb*

To attribute or assign causal responsibility to a person or thing. *Ascribing* something to someone is acknowledging their responsibility or creation of it.

> *This work has been ascribed to Rousseau, but his authorship now seems uncertain.*

aspersion *(uh-SPUR-zhun)*, *noun*

False accusation; slander. To cast an *aspersion* on another is to make an unfair or untrue statement about his conduct or character.

> *I will not allow you to cast these aspersions on a man whose career has been so distinguished.*

assertion *(uh-SUR-shun)*, *noun*

A positive statement or claim. An *assertion* is something claimed straightforwardly, without support of evidence or logical justification.

> *Your assertion that my car was at the scene of the crime has no basis in fact.*

assiduously *(uh-SID-joo-us-lee)*, *adverb*

Constantly; unceasingly in effort; persistently. Someone who is diligent and persistent is *assiduous*. Someone who works unremittingly and attentively works *assiduously*.

*Karen worked assiduously to complete her final
project, but was still one day late.*

audacious *(aw-DAY-shuss)*, *adjective*

Brazen, daring, or fearless. *Audacious* refers to bold,
unrestrained, uncompromising behavior. It often carries a
sense of bending accepted rules or disregarding prevalent
standards.

> *His audacious behavior at the family reunion
> shocked even his brothers and sisters.*

augmentation *(awg-men-TAY-shun)*, *noun*

The process of increasing in extent, size, or scope.   The
broadening, extension, or increase of something is that
thing's *augmentation.*

> *He had hoped to bring in enough money with the
> second job, but even this augmentation of his income
> was not enough for him to meet the payments.*

auspices *(AWS-pis-uz)*, *noun*

Support, encouragement, or patronage. *Auspices* is generally
used with "under" To operate under the auspices of an
organization is to act with that organization's
encouragement or permission.

> *The emergency food shipments were delivered under
> the auspices of the United Nations.*

auspicious *(aws-PISH-us)*, *adjective*

Promising; seemingly favorable or likrly to be accompanied
by good fortune. *Auspicious* is usually used to describe
encouraging signals or reasons for optimism at the
beginning of an undertaking.

> *The trip did not begin auspiciously; our car broke
> down within an hour.*

austere *(aw-STEER), adjective*

Severe in appearance or nature; self disciplined or strict to a high degree. An *austere* person is self-controlled and somber. That which is without ornamentation or luxury is *austere*.

> *Despite his austere public image, the activist indulged a secret passion for expensive, wild nights out on the town.*

autonomous *(aw-TAWN-uh-mus) adjective*

Operating in an independent manner. An *autonomous* person or institution is one acting independently and free from restraint or control.

> *The question of when--or whether--the region is to become an autonomous nation is a difficult one.*

avail *(uh-VAYL), verb*

To be of benefit or use. Someone whose actions are to no *avail* acts in vain.

> *In November, we decided to avail ourselves of the opportunity for a vacation.*

avant-garde *(ahv-ahnt GARD), adjective*

Relating to the latest trends, especially in the world of art; of a new or experimental nature. The term is French for "fore guard", or furthest from the line of battle. The *avant-garde* is the latest, most advanced work in a field, especially in the arts. As a noun, *avant garde* refers to the group doing this work.

> *Milton found keeping pace with avant-garde work in sculpture both challenging and rewarding for his own work.*

avarice *(AV-er-iss), noun*
Great desire for riches. *Avarice* is extreme greed. Those who hoard wealth compulsively can be said to be avaricious.

> *Although Matthew was an extremely successful businessman, avarice was certainly not in his nature.*

avowal *(uh-VOW-uhl), noun*
An open admission or statement. To avow is to declare openly, so an *avowal* is an unconcealed declaration or confession.

> *He had run as a Democrat for over thirty years, so his avowal of support for the Republican ticket shocked many supporters.*

Babbitt *(BAB-it), noun*
A person who clings to narrow-minded, materialistic ideals of the middle class. Sinclair Lewis' novel *Babbitt* has as its main character a man whose conventional ideals of success and business lead to self-satisfaction and indifference to higher human values.

> *Jerome may not be the most open-minded businessman, but he's no Babbitt.*

baccalaureate *(bak-uh-LOR-ee-it), noun*
The degree awarded upon completion of an undergraduate course of study. A *baccalaureate*, also called a bachelor's degree, is the degree given to a college graduate. A *baccalaureate* is also a farewell address to a graduating class.

> *I received my baccalaureate in 1983 from Brandeis University.*

balderdash *(BALL-der-dash), noun*
Nonsense; a ridiculous idea or suggestion. To say an idea is *balderdash* is to dismiss it as senseless, idle, or worthless. *Balderdash* is used almost exclusively to describe writing or speech.

> *He went as far as to suggest the works of Shakespeare had been written by Queen Elizabeth, as if further examination of that balderdash would help his cause.*

bandy *(BAN-dee), verb*
To exchange or pass back and forth. Trading words or blows is often referred to as *bandying*. To exchange witticisms or insults is to *bandy* them about.

> *The two sides bandied threats and accusations for months, but it was clear that neither nation wanted war.*

baneful *(BAYN-ful), adjective*
Extremely harmful, ruinous, or destructive. Bane is anything that spoils or destroys utterly; *baneful*, then, means deadly and likely to cause ruin. The word is often used for dramatic effect and so is likely to describe that which should be considered deadly.

> *His baneful influence on the younger man in the squad was the cause of all the misdeeds we are examining.*

barbarous *(BAR-ber-us), adjective*
Uncivilized or primitive; characterized by brutality or savagery. To say that something or someone is *barbarous* is to say that it is crude and lacks refinement. *Barbarous* treatment is uncivilized or even cruel and brutal.

> *Their captivity was marked by barbarous living conditions, psychological abuse, and little or no*

no news of outside events.

barrage *(buh-ROZH)*, *noun*
Concentrated outpouring or volley. A *barrage* is an overwhelming torrent of something, usually words, blows, or projectiles. The word was originally used only in a military sense.

> *The defense attorney subjected the witness to a barrage of questions about the events of that night.*

beatitude *(bee-AT-it-tood)*, *noun*
Highest possible blessedness or contentment. Also: Any of the declarations ("Blessed are . . .") made by Jesus in the biblical account of his Sermon on the Mount (usually capitalized). *Beatitude* comes from the Latin for "perfect happiness."

> *His translation of Christ's Beatitudes cast new light on the familiar declarations.*

bedraggled *(bee-DRAG-eld)*, *adjective*
Harried or in a condition of disarray; unkempt; dirty and limp. A person who has just walked a long way through mud and rain could be said to be *bedraggled*.

> *A group of bedraggled orphans stood outside begging by the flickering gaslight.*

befuddle *(bee-FUD-il)*, *verb*
To confuse or perplex. To *befuddle* is to mystify or confuse, as with bewildering arguments or misleading statements.

> *His vague account of strange doings in the woods succeeded in befuddling the policemen, and probably saved him a traffic ticket.*

belated *(bee-LAY-ted), adjective*
Late or tardy; delayed. *Belated* refers to anything past due.

> *Jane sent a belated birthday card, but still felt guilty about forgetting her mother's birthday.*

beleaguered *(bee-LEEG-erd), adjective*
Embattled; constantly confronted with obstacles. To *beleaguer* is, literally, to beseige or surround with an army for the purpose of harrassment. When we say someone is *beleaguered*, we mean that he is beset with many troubles.

> *The beleaguered financier even considered bankruptcy, but vowed to fight on.*

belie *(bee-LYE) verb*
To disprove or demonstrate to be false; to contradict appearances. To say something *belies* something else is to say that it gives evidence of a contrary state of affairs.

> *His unsteady walk and slurred speech belied his insistence of having consumed no alcohol at the party.*

belligerent *(buh-LIJ-er-ent), adjective*
Aggresive or pugnacious; eager to instigate a fight. *Belligerent* is rooted in the Latin word for "war."

> *Don became overbearing and belligerent with his employees after his divorce, causing many of them to resign.*

bemused *(bee-MYOOZD), adjective*
The quality of being bewildered, perplexed, or lost in reflection. A person who is preoccupied or confused by

something is *bemused*.

> *Victor stared bemused at the photograph of his father in full military dress--a man he had never thought of in quite that way.*

benediction *(ben-i-DIK-shun), noun*

A formal blessing, an expression of good wishes. The most common sense of *benediction* has to do with the invocation of God's blessing at the end of a church service, but the word can also mean the expression of goodwill from one person to another.

> *As the priest pronounced the benediction, Julia looked around the pew for her coat but could not find it.*

benevolent *(be-NEV-i-lent), adjective*

Marked by a tendency to do well toward others; kindly. A *benevolent* act is one in service to another. The word is derived from the Latin for "good wishes."

> *There is a benevolent side to Mark one would not expect to see in a man so apparently cold.*

benighted *(bee-NYT-ed), adjective*

Ignorant or unenlightened. Also: Lost in night or darkness. A person in intellectual or moral darkness is said to be *benighted*. A culture or time that is considered primitive or crude can also be said to be benighted.

> *It was a benighted era of superstition and folly, yet its problems were not all that different from ours.*

bequeath *(bee-QUEETH), verb*

Bestow by means of a will. *Bequeath* is often used metaphorically to describe something handed down to a group of people from those of a past era.

More than anything else, it is the language we speak, bequeathed to us by Byron and Shakespeare and Milton and a legion of others, that binds us to the English and them to us.

bereaved (bih-REEVD), *adjective or noun*

In a state of mourning; deeply sorrowful because of the loss of a loved one. As a noun, *bereaved* refers to the person in mourning (and is usually preceded by *the*).

> *The most difficult part of Father Maurice's job was providing solace for the bereaved in his parish.*

beseech *(bih-SEECH), verb*

To entreat, implore, or request earnestly. *Beseech* is a formal verb used to request something. In contemporary use, it reflects either great (or even fawning) politeness or urgency of the highest order.

> *We beseech you, Mr. Prime Minister: think twice before committing the lives of so many of our countrymen to this cause.*

bestial *(BESS-chul), adjective*

Of, pertaining to, or reminiscent of beasts. Something is *bestial* if it exhibits savagery or brutality.

> *The colonel's bestial treatment of the prisoners of war was in violation of the Geneva Convention.*

bestow *(bih-STOW), verb*

To confer or give. One *bestows* an award, honor, or degree. The verb is usually followed by *on* or *upon*.

> *Though he lacked formal education, several universities had bestowed honorary degrees on Mr. Goldfarb.*

bete noire *(bett NWAHR), noun*
Something one does not like or finds extremely fearful.
Bete noire is French for "black beast."

> *Jean got A's in all subjects except geometry, her
> longtime bete noire.*

bigamy *(BIG-uh-mee), noun*
The crime of taking marriage vows while still legally
married to someone else. *Bigamy* is an offense involving
illicit marriage, but it also describes other ecclesiastical
violations of religious law regarding marital status.

> *By marrying June before her divorce was finalized,
> Stanley was technically guilty of bigamy.*

bilateral *(bye-LAT-er-uhl), adjective*
Involving or pertaining to both sides of something. A
bilateral agreement is one that affects and is binding upon
both parties.

> *It is useless to try to settle such issues in our
> legislature; only a bilateral trade agreement will
> resolve our disputes with that nation.*

bilk *(bilk), verb*
To swindle or cheat. Someone who defrauds a person or
institution of funds or goods *bilks* the victim.

> *The accountant, investigators learned, had been
> bilking the company of nearly a quarter of a million
> dollars a year.*

binary *(BYE-nair-ee), adjective*
Constructed of two elements; of or pertaining to two. A
binary number system is one with two digits; zero and

one.

> *The decimal number 2 would be written as 10 in binary notation, since one times two to the first power plus zero times two to the zero power equals two.*

biogenesis *(bye-oh-JEN-ih-siss), noun*
The process of life arising from other living things. *Biogenesis*, a scientific word, was coined by T.H. Huxley in 1870.

> *Biogenesis involves an unending regenerative cycle of life and death.*

bipolar *(bye-POE-luhr), adjective*
Possessing two sides or poles; marked by diametrically opposed extremes. A *bipolar* relationship is one between two opposites or counterparts.

> *Frank's behavior on the job was generally unremarkable, but we later learned that his severe mood swings were symptoms of a bipolar personality disorder.*

blase *(blah-ZAY), adjective*
Unimpressed; bored. Someone who has seen too much of something to become excited about it can be said to be *blase*.

> *I told Jim that he stood a very good chance of being fired this week, but to tell you the truth he seemed rather blase about the whole thing.*

blather *(BLATH-er), verb*
To gabble or talk ridiculously. Someone who *blathers* is prone to talk nonsense or discuss meaningless issues for extended periods.

We tried to leave the party, but Mark insisted on blathering endlessly to the hostess about his new car.

blithe *(blithe), adjective*
Cheerful or merry in disposition; carefree or indifferent. A person who is *blithe* is unconcerned with petty cares or problems.

Rod dismissed the accountant's objections with a blithe wave of the hand.

bludgeon *(BLUD-jun), verb and noun*
To beat. As a noun, a *bludgeon* is a short, heavy stick. To *bludgeon* someone is to beat or strike him with a similar instrument.

The detectives concluded that the victim had been bludgeoned repeatedly with a metal pipe.

bluster *(BLUS-ter), verb*
To threaten swaggeringly or issue extravagant threats. *Bluster* is related to the same old word from which *blow* (as in "the wind blows") is derived.

He seems fierce at first, but you must remember that he depends largely on blustering to get his way.

bohemian *(bo-HEE-mee-un), adjective*
Unconventional; reminiscent of a lifestyle free of the restraints and concerns of mainstream society. To say someone is *bohemian* is to say he is a free thinker and lives without much concern for the inhibitions associated with the workaday world.

Jane loved Carl, but was unprepared to share in his bohemian way of life.

bombast *(BOM-bast), noun*
Haughty, overblown or pompous talk or writing. Someone who engages in *bombast* indulges a taste for an exaggerated rhetorical style.

> *We expected a compelling argument from our attorney, but he came to court offering little more than bombast.*

bona fide *(BOE-nuh fyde), adjective*
Actual; genuine. Something that is *bona fide* is indisputably legitimate.

> *Let's treat the discovery of this supposed newfound masterpiece with a healthy skepticism; after all, there are less than twenty bona fide Vermeers known to exist in the whole world.*

boorish *(BOO-rish), adjective*
Offensive; lacking manners, civility, or consideration. A *boorish* person is one completely unfamiliar with social graces.

> *Everett's boorish behavior at the party was completely out of character for him.*

botanical *(buh-TAN-ih-kull), adjective*
Of or pertaining to plant life. A *botanical* garden is one that features a wide variety of plant life. The word comes from the Greek *botanikos*, meaning "herb."

> *Martin's botanical survey of rainforest plants required a series of trips to Borneo.*

bovine *(BO-vine), adjective*
Dull, unresponsive, or slow. *Bovine* means, literally, "of or pertaining to cows."

> *Are we to expect breakthroughs from such a bovine group of scientific followers?*

braggadocio *(brag-uh-DOCE-ee-oo), noun*
Bragging or meaningless boasting. *Braggadocio* can refer both to actual boasting or to a person who engages in it.

> *It appears that the dire warnings we received some weeks back were nothing more than braggadocio.*

brandish *(BRAN-dish), verb*
To flourish or shake menacingly or ostentatiously. Something can be *brandished* either out of defiance, as a warning of potential future harm, or out of pride, as a sign of status.

> *He brandished a revolver; the room suddenly fell silent.*

brash *(brash), adjective*
Impudent; hasty. Something done impetuously and quickly is *brash*. *Brash* can also refer to a certain zesty or irreverent quality that may be seen as refreshing.

> *The action you have taken is brash; you will regret your recklessness.*

brassy *(BRASS-ee), adjective*
Brazen; cheap or showy. *Brassy* can also refer to a bold, outgoing nature.

> *The promotional campaign struck a brassy, daring tone that instantly won consumer attention.*

bravado *(bruh-VA-do), noun*
An open show of bravery. That which is characterized by a display of boldness shows *bravado*.

> *The mayor's swaggering attitude of bravado was of little help when the town was finally attacked.*

brevity *(BREV-ih-tee), noun*
Shortness. Someone who writes with *brevity* writes in a way that is terse and to the point.

> *Paine's argument was stated with such brevity and passion that within one short month of its publication it seemed every colonist was in favor or independence from Britain.*

brunt *(brunt), noun*
The primary impact of a blow. The *brunt* of an attack is the point of its main force.

> *If there is a war, rest assured that it is our country that will be asked to bear the brunt of it.*

brusque *(brusk), adjective*
Short; abrupt or curt in manner. A person who discusses things impatiently or with shortness is said to be *brusque*.

> *Her brusque exterior put Tom off at first, but he later discussed many imprtant issues with Ann in depth.*

bugaboo *(BUG-uh-boo), noun*
An object of fear. Something that causes worry or dismay is a *bugaboo*.

*I hope you're not going to be swayed by the old
bugaboo that changing a package design is a sure
way to kill a product.*

bumptious *(BUMP-shuss), adjective*
Overbearing or crudely assertive. Someone who is
bumptious is overly pushy or impertinent.

*We had difficulty crossing the border because Nan
got into a squabble with a bumptious border guard.*

bureaucracy *(byoo-ROK-ruh-see), noun*
The concentration of power and authority in administrative
bodies. Also: an administrative body. *Bureaucracy* is often
characterized by adherence to routine and lack of
innovation.

*As the company grew, the entrenched bureaucracies
in the accounting and finance departments gained
more and more influence.*

bygone *(BYE-gone), adjective and noun*
Something gone by. A *bygone* occurrence is one that took
place in the past. Used as a noun, a *bygone* refers to an
event that took place long enough ago to be seen in the
proper perspective, as in the phrase "Let bygones be
bygones."

*The inn calls to mind a bygone era of Southern
hospitality.*

calvary *(CAL-vuh-ree), noun*
A scene of intense anguish (named for the hill on which
Jesus Christ was crucified, Calvary). *Calvary* is frequently
confused with *cavalry* (see *cavalry* below), but their
meanings are entirely different.

Herbert faced his own private calvary after his wife

told him she wanted a divorce.

canard *(kuh-NARD), noun*
A fabrication or unfounded story. Someone who spreads a rumor he knows to be false and harmful would be guilty of circulating a *canard*.

> *The claim that the president of the company is likely to resign soon has been throughly discredited, but you will still hear some members of the opposition spreading the canard.*

candor *(KAN-duhr), noun*
Openness or honesty. Someone who speaks directly or openly, without equivocation or doubletalk, can be said to speak with *candor*.

> *Let me say with all candor that I did not look forward to coming here today.*

canonical *(kuh-NON-ih-kuhl), adjective*
In accordance with or conforming to established (church) law. *Also:* accepted as belonging within a body of work (especially the Bible). Orthodox behavior can be said to be *canonical*.

> *The canonical requirements of the sect were stringent and difficult to obey.*

capacious *(kuh-PAY-shus), adjective*
Capable of holding a great deal of something. Something that is spacious or capable of encompassing a large quantity of an item can be said to be *capacious*.

> *Don't let his show of ignorance fool you; he has a capacious memory and a strong eye for detail.*

capitulate *(kuh-PIT-yoo-late), verb*
To accede to a demand for surrender. Someone who yields
a point under dispute can be said to *capitulate* to the
other party.

> *The ambassador had been instructed to show
> flexibility on cultural exchanges, but not to
> capitulate when it came to trade issues.*

capricious *(kuh-PREE-shuss)*
Characterized by a whimsical attitude. A person who acts
impulsively or unpredictably can be said to be *capricious.*

> *Given his capricious approach to life, it is not
> surprising that Andrew never settled into one field of
> employment.*

captious *(KAP-shuss), adjective*
Extremely critical; likely to find fault. A person who makes
many criticisms about petty matters can be said to be
captious.

> *Myra had shown great tolerance throughout her stay,
> but when Mr. Clements subjected her to a captious
> interrogation about her academic career, she decided
> to leave.*

cardinal *(KAR-dih-nul), adjective*
Primarily important; vital; prominent. A *cardinal* sin is one
of great seriousness. As a noun, *cardinal* can refer to a
number of things or people regarded as primary or
important, including a kind of high official in the Roman
Catholic church.

> *Whatever you do, remember the cardinal rule we
> have in this house about avoiding the subject of
> religion.*

caricature *(KARE-ihk-uh-choor), noun*
A grotesquely or absurdly exaggerated representation.
Political cartoons are the most common examples of
caricature, but many modes of expression make use of the
form's distortion and contrast.

> *The paintings of Toulouse-Lautrec are often rooted in
> caricature, but they are more than mere cartoons.*

carpe diem *(KAR-pay DEE-uhm) (Latin)*
Relish the present and take joy now in the pleasure of
life, rather than focusing on the future. *Carpe diem* is
Latin for "seize the day."

> *His final admonition was to live life to the fullest--a
> carpe diem he seemed to have heeded rarely himself.*

carte blanche *(kart blonsh), noun*
Unrestricted power, access, or privilege; permission to act
entirely as one wishes. *Carte blanche* is from the French
for "blank document'; the essential meaning is that one is
free to "write one's own ticket."

> *Jean had carte blance during her first month or so
> as office manager, but the vice-president eventually
> came to supervise her much more closely.*

cartel *(kar-TELL), noun*
A group assembled with the objective of establishing mutual
control over prices, production, and marketing of goods by
the members. While a *cartel* is usually a group of
representatives from independent business organizations, the
term can also refer to a coalition of political figures united
for a particular cause.

> *The oil cartel had succeeded in driving world energy
> prices up significantly.*

caste *(kast), noun*
A social class marked by strong hereditary and cultural ties.
Caste also refers to the strict set of social boundaries and
customs determined by birth within Hindu society.

> *When Roland married the daughter of a shopkeeper,
> he was accused by some of having betrayed his
> caste.*

catalyst *(KAT-uh-list), noun*
That which initiates a process or event and is itself
unaffected. *Catalyst* has a technical meaning in chemistry,
but in general usage it refers to a person or thing that
sets off a new sequence of events while remaining
uninvolved in those events.

> *The film served as a catalyst for Peter; he began
> keeping a journal regularly soon after he saw it.*

catch-22 *(KATCH-twen-tee-too), noun*
An impossible situation in which one is presented with
logically contradictory options. A demand that one call the
phone repair service from the very telephone that is out of
order, for instance, could be regarded as a *catch-22*. (The
phrase is drawn from Joseph Heller's novel of the same
name.)

> *Mr. Brown's lighthearted memo issued a playful
> catch-22: he was only to be scheduled for meetings
> taking place during those days he planned to be out
> of town.*

catharsis *(kuh-THAR-siss), noun*
An emotional purging. *Catharsis* is a cleansing of the mind
or soul usually initiated by a supreme insight or challenge.

> *Olivier's character undergoes a remarkable catharsis
> in the final twenty minutes of the film.*

caustic *(KOSS-tick), adjective*
Corrosive or capable of burning. Something is *caustic* if it can eat away at something else. A person is *caustic* if he speaks sharply and maliciously.

> *The caustic nature of Jane's speech caused all the members to reexamine their support of her candidacy.*

cavalcade *(KAV-uhl-kade), noun*
A procession, especially one involving people on horses or in vehicles. A *cavalcade* can refer to a parade or to anything that is to be displayed with great pageantry.

> *The president served as host to a cavalcade of visiting dignitaries.*

cavalier *(KAV-uh-leer), adjective*
Unconcerned with what is considered important; nonchalantly unengaged, especially with regard to serious matters. A reckless or inattentive person charged with responsibility in affairs of importance can be said to be *cavalier*.

> *His cavalier attitude toward financial management may be his company's undoing.*

cavalry *(CAV-ul-ree), noun*
A group of soldiers on horseback. *Cavalry* is frequently confused with *calvary* (see *calvary* above), but their meanings are entirely different.

> *After three days of delay, the cavalry finally came to the rescue.*

caveat emptor *(KAH-vee-ott EMP-tore) (Latin)*
"Let the buyer beware." *Caveat emptor* is a Latin phrase
warning that swindles and misrepresentation are common
in the world of commerce. (A caveat is a warning.) The
term can also mean that goods are sold without warranty.

> *Fran bought the goods at her own peril and*
> *regretted her act:* caveat emptor!

cavil *(KAV-ihl), verb*
To find fault in trivial matters or raise petty objections. As
a noun, *cavil* can mean a trivial objection.

> *Susan cavilled for some time about the lateness of*
> *the milk delivery, but since it was only a matter of*
> *minutes, she eventually gave in and paid the bill.*

celerity *(sub-LAIR-ih-tee), noun*
Speed; swiftness of action or motion. *Celerity* comes from
the same Latin root as accelerate.

> *I will carry out your orders with celerity, sir.*

celibacy *(SELL-ih-bus-see), noun*
The quality of being chaste; the act of abstaining from
sexual activity. For instance, someone who remains
unmarried in order to follow a religious calling is said to
commit to a lifestyle of *celibacy*.

> *Although he took Holy Orders, David eventually*
> *found that he could not live a life of celibacy and*
> *left the priesthood.*

censure *(SEN-sher), noun*
A show of disapproval or blame. *Censure* is formal rebuke
or stern reproof.

*You could not have acted as you did without
expecting censure from this organization.*

cessation *(sess-SAY-shun), noun*
The act of drawing to a close. *Cessation* is the process of
ceasing or reaching a point of abatement.

*Continued diplomatic effort may well bring about a
cessation of hostilities.*

chagrin *(shuh-GRIN), noun*
The emotion of humiliation or embarrassment arising from
disheartening experience. To show *chagrin* is to give
evidence of disappointment and disquiet with oneself.

*Much to my chagrin, my application was rejected
instantly.*

charismatic *(kare-ihz-MAT-ik), adjective*
Possessing a special quality associated with leadership,
authority, confidence, and overall personal appeal. While
we generally use *charismatic* in reference to a person, the
word also refers to certain Christian sects and ideas that
emphasize demonstrative or ecstatic worship.

*The charismatic salesman seemed to sell himself as
much as his product.*

charlatan *(SHAR-luh-tun), noun*
A fake or humbug. A *charlatan* falsely claims to possess a
given level of status, skils, or knowledge.

*The defendant, it has been claimed, is a charlatan
and a liar--but where is the evidence for this?*

chimerical *(kih-MARE-ih-kull), adjective*
Fanciful, imaginary, or unreal. A *chimerical* event is one
that seems dreamlike or surrealistic.

> *A chimerical landscape greeted those brave enough to
> emerge from the ship.*

chivalrous *(SHIV-uhl-russ), adjective*
Honorable; in keeping with a code of behavior reminiscent
of that followed by medieval knights. *Chivalrous* applies
especially to courteousness and/or consideration toward
women, the poor, or the vanquished.

> *Those who expected a barbarian were surprised to find
> the renegade leader both even-tempered and chivalrous
> in bearing.*

circumlocution *(sir-kum-lo-CUE-shun), noun*
Overwordy and indirect language. Language that is
overblown and tedious is considered *circumlocution*.

> *The student's use of circumlocution lengthened his
> report, but lowered his grade.*

circumvent *(SIR-kum-vent), verb*
To evade by means of artful contrivance. Someone who
circumvents a regulation has not broken it in the strict
sense, but found a gray area or loophole within which to
operate. Similarly, to *circumvent* someone's authority is to
maneuver around him.

> *In circumventing the will of the board of directors,
> the CEO knew he was taking a risk.*

citadel *(SIT-uh-del), noun*
A stronghold; literally, a strategically positioned fortress in
control of a town or city. Something that is forfeited
against attack or adversity may be referred to

metaphorically as a *citadel*.

> *Gentlemen, this business is our citadel, and we must be prepared to defend it as such.*

clairvoyance *(klare-VOY-uhnce), noun*
Supernatural perceptive skills. *Clairvoyance* (from the French for "clear sight") refers to the ability to perceive things normally out of the range of human intuition.

> *Michael claimed to have clairvoyance, and even held a few playful "seances," but no one took his claims seriously.*

clamorous *(KLAM-uhr-uss), adjective*
Loud; expressively vehement. A *clamorous* crowd is noisy and demanding; a *clamor* is a loud outcry.

> *The throngs in the street roared with clamorous applause.*

clandestine *(klan-DESS-tin), adjective*
Kept hidden; secreted away from authorities or public observance. A *clandestine* object is one that is concealed for a purpose hidden from general view.

> *The message reached the resistance movement by means of a coded broadcast heard in hundreds of clandestine radios around the country.*

clemency *(KLEM-uhn-see), noun*
Forbearance or mercy toward a wrongdoer or opponent. To show *clemency* is to be lenient in cases where circumstances warrant.

> *The governor's show of clemency for Callahan may come back to haunt him at election time.*

coalesce *(ko-uh-LESS), verb*
To unite or grow into a single whole. Disparate groups that *coalesce* for a single cause (thus forming a coalition) put aside their differences or separate goals to present a united front.

> *No amount of pleading from Jones could convince the two unions to coalesce.*

codify *(KOD-ih-fy), verb*
To reduce to the form of a code. To *codify* a series of positions is to systematize them, setting them down into distinct rules and guidelines.

> *It is high time we codified the existing maze of tax regulations.*

cogent *(KOE-junt), adjective*
Compelling or convincing. Something that appeals effectively to the intellect or reason is said to be *cogent*.

> *I must admit that my counterpart has put forward a cogent argument in defense of his client.*

cogitate *(KOJ-ih-tate), verb*
To ponder or ruminate. To *cogitate* about something is to take careful stock of it or meditate upon it closely.

> *Steven was ready to give up; no amount of cogitation, it seemed, would yield a solution.*

cognition *(kog-NISH-un), noun*
Perception; the process of knowing. *Cognition* can also mean "knowledge."

> *The process of cognition develops with amazing rapidity over the first two years of life.*

cohort (KO-hort), noun

An associate or companion with whom one is united through common experience. *Cohort* originally referred to one of the ten divisions of a Roman legion, consisting of men who had developed strong ties of comradeship.

Because Mark and his cohorts had grown up together in the town, leaving for different colleges was quite difficult.

colloquial (kuh-LO-kwee-ul), adjective

In common conversational use. *Colloquial* is used to describe breezy, informal communication, either written or spoken. A *colloquialism* is a common phrase or expression of a conversational or informal nature.

You cannot expect a college president to take seriously a letter so colloquial in tone.

collusion (kuh-LOO-zhun), noun

A conspiratorial or secret understanding entered into for an illicit or fraudulent end. To enter into *collusion* with someone is to join with him in a secret plot or strategy.

The leaders were arraigned on price collusion in violation of anti-trust laws.

comely (KUM-lee), adjective

Pleasing or attractive. Also; appropriate. A *comely* appearance is one that is fetching or inviting.

Jane is comely, but her mother fears that the men she attracts will not make her happy.

commensurate (kuh-MEN-sir-it), adjective

Having an equal measure; of equivalent duration or extent. Something that is *commensurate* with something else is of a proper scope or size by comparison.

Michael received a raise commensurate with his performance.

commiserate *(kuh-MIZ-uh-rate), verb*
To share in another's sorrow or disappointment. *Commiserate* comes from the Latin roots for "with" and "pitiable."

Jane and Anita commiserated with Frank over the failure of the business.

compendious *(kum-PEN-dee-us), adjective*
Comprised of all necessary or essential components, yet concise. Something that is *compendious* (usually a piece of writing) deals with all important matters in a tight, succinct format.

The new desk encyclopedia is compendious but typographically unattractive..

complaisant *(kum-PLAY-zunt), adjective*
Eager to please; agreeable. *Complaisant* is frequently confused with the similar-sounding "complacent," which means "self-satisfied."

After months of personality problems with Trish, Fran suddenly found her quite complaisant.

comport *(kum-PORT), verb*
To behave in a particular fashion. Also: to stand in harmonious relation. This second sense of *comport* is usually followed by "with."

That does not comport with the facts, counselor.

compunction *(kum-PUNK-shun), noun*
Unrest or self-dissatisfaction arising out of a feeling of guiltiness. A *compunction* is a sensation of remorse or uncertainty about a decision or course of action.

> *I will sign her dismissal notice myself without compunction; she is easily the most incompetent salesperson I have ever worked with.*

concerted *(kun-SUR-tid), adjective*
Mutually devised or planned. A *concerted* effort is one that features mutual effort toward an established goal.

> *The two made a concerted effort to get Vivian to change her mind, but she was resolute.*

concourse *(KON-korse), noun*
An assembly of a large number of people. A *concourse* can also be a large open area meant to accommodate public gatherings.

> *He looked all around the concourse, but could not see Robin.*

concurrence *(kun-KER-runce), noun*
The condition of being in agreement. To concur is to agree, so a *concurrence* is in effect when two or more people have "signed on" to a given idea, plan, or judgment.

> *I will proceed with the acquisition; as president, I do not require anyone else's concurrence.*

confabulate *(kun-FAB-yoo-late), verb*
To chat or talk informally. *Confabulate* derives from the Latin for "to have a conversation with." (*Confabulation* also has a technical meaning in psychiatry: the process by which people invent and believe stories to fill mental gaps

due to memory loss. *Confabulation* is sometimes used in this sense in general discourse to describe extravagant storytelling.)

> *"I have no time to confabulate," the actor exclaimed melodramatically before leaving.*

confluence *(KON-flu-ence), noun*
A point of meeting or flowing together. Literally, a *confluence* is the point at which two rivers join. The word has been expanded significantly through metaphorical use.

> *It is on the issue of human spiritual growth that the two philosophies find their confluence.*

congenial *(kun-JEEN-ee-ul), adjective*
Having similar habits or tastes; temperamentally suitable. *Congenial* surroundings are those that yield a sense of being pleasant and inviting. (*Congenial* is sometimes confused with *congenital*; see below.)

> *He found Jane a congenial hostess: easy to engage in conversation and knowledgeable on topics of interest to others.*

congenital *(kun-JEN-it-ul), adjective*
Present or existing from birth. A *congenital* disease or condition can be inherited, or can result from environmental influences (usually influences on growth within the womb).

> *The young child suffered from a congenital heart defect.*

conjecture *(kun-JEK-shur), noun*
Speculation based on inconclusive data or on evidence that is not complete. A *conjecture* can be considered a "best guess" unsupported by fact or observation.

> *The item that appeared in your column of December 16th is based totally on conjecture, and is extremely misleading.*

conjure *(KON-jur), verb*
To summon or bring about (as if by supernatural means).
Someone who *conjures* up an image of something brings it
to mind in a vivid way.

> *I cannot simply conjure up the figures you are
> looking for; the project will take some time.*

connotation *(kon-uh-TAY-shun), noun*
An implication beyond literal meaning; an unspoken
suggestion. To connote is to suggest something implicitly;
accordingly, a *connotation* is a secondary meaning
discernable "beneath the surface."

> *His article on race relations uses several phrases
> that carry unfortunate connotations.*

consanguineous *(con-san-GWIN-ee-us), adjective*
Related by blood; of common lineage. Two people or
entities that are *consanguineous* are commonly descended.
The word derives from the Latin roots for "with" and
"blood."

> *The two brothers learned of their consanguineous
> relationship after a series of blood tests.*

consecrate *(KON-si-krate), verb*
To proclaim as sacred; to set aside or declare to be holy.
By extension, to *consecrate* oneself to a given goal is to
commit to it with a conviction in keeping with strong faith.

> *Lincoln's words, more than any other action after
> the carnage, served to consecrate the battlefield at
> Gettysburg.*

consortium *(kon-SOR-tee-um), noun*
A union, partnership, or alliance, especially one among
financial or business entities. *Consortium* also has a legal
meaning related to the rights of married persons, but use
in this sense is rare.

> *Mr. Sparks represented a consortium of firms.*

consternation *(kon-ster-NAY-shun), noun*
Dismay; sudden amazement or alarm. To show
consternation is to display amazement or confusion at a
turn of events.

> *The stock's sudden drop in price caused a good deal
> of consternation in the market.*

construe *(con-STROO), verb*
To translate or analyze structurally. To *construe* something
is to come to a conclusion on its meaning based on
review of it.

> *This clause is not to be construed as granting any
> rights of partnership.*

consummate *(KON-sum-mate), verb*
To complete or finalize; to bring to a point of finality or a
desired end. To *consummate* something is to bring it to its
point of fulfillment. When we speak of a marriage's
consummation, we refer to the married couple's
establishment of a sexual relationship. Business agreements
and contracts are also *consummated*.

> *The real estate agent consummating the deal realized
> a substantial commission.*

contemptuous *(kun-TEMP-choo-us), adjective*
Feeling disdain or scorn. A *contemptuous* act is one that
flies in the face of established procedures or traditions.

> *The defendant's contemptuous behavior on the stand
> was, amazingly, overlooked by the judge.*

contravene *(kon-truh-VEEN), verb*
To go against or deny. A person who opposes something
by action or argument can be said to *contravene* that
thing.

> *The orders I left were to be contravened by no one
> but the colonel.*

contrition *(kun-TRISH-un), noun*
Sadness or remorse over past wrong actions. Technically, *contrition* is one of the conditions for absolution from sin for members of the Roman Catholic church. The word is also used in a broader secular sense.

> *He showed not the lest contrition for his acts, even when confronted by his victims.*

contrivance *(kun-TRY-vunce), noun*
A device or artful means of acquiring or performing something. *Contrivance* may refer to an actual mechanical object, or, more darkly, to a plot or scheme.

> *The false expense report totals--a rather obvious contrivance--were discovered well before the embezzlement took place.*

contumely *(kon-TYOO-muh-lee), noun*
A rude display in speech or deed; contemptuous behavior. *Contumely* can also mean humiliating derision.

> *No matter how long he had held the grudge against Aaron, his contumely at the wedding was uncalled for.*

convalescence *(kon-vuh-LESS-unce), noun*
The process of regaining one's health after an illness. *Convalescence* is derived from the Latin for "to grow stronger."

> *Her convalescence was impeded by the primitive medical facilities on the island.*

convivial *(kun-VIV-ee-ul), adjective*
Amiable; given to feasting, drinking, and socializing. To say something (especially a gathering of people) is *convivial* is to say it is festive and sociable.

> *The party, which was originally quite stuffy-feeling, took on a more convivial nature as the evening wore on.*

convocation *(kon-vo-KAY-shun)*, *noun*
An assembly of people gathered in response to a summons.
Convocation also has a technical meaning within the
Episcopal church: a gathering of laity requested by church
officials.

> *The address Mr. Freling gave at the convocation*
> *challenged all graduates to excel.*

convoluted *(kon-vuh-LOO-tid)*, *adjective*
Complicated and twisted; intermingled or intimately folded
together. *Convoluted* means, literally, folded into a coil or
spiral; it is more commonly used to express an extreme
state of complication and/or interdependency.

> *His argument, though perhaps sound to an expert in*
> *the field, seemed extremely convoluted to me.*

copious *(KO-pee-us)*, *adjective*
Abundant; large or generous in extent. That which is broad
in scope or abundant is *copious*.

> *The winter's copious rainfall was welcomed by area*
> *farmers.*

coquettish *(ko-KET-ish)*, *adjective*
Given to flirting. *Coquettish* is almost always used to
describe women rather than men.

> *Little Amy's coquettish display was noted with*
> *amusement by all.*

corroborate *(kuh-ROB-uh-rate)*, *verb*
To confirm or increase in certainty. In a legal case, new
evidence or testimony that supports previous theories is
said to *corroborate* those theories.

> *The maid saw me here at 10 p.m.; she can*
> *corroborate my story.*

covenant *(KUH-vuh-nent), noun*
A binding agreement entered into by two or more. According to the Bible, a *covenant* was made between the ancient Israelites and Jehovah.

>*To James the arrangement was an informal understanding, but to Michael it was a holy covenant.*

covert *(KO-vert), adjective*
Secret; covered over. Something that is *covert* is concealed or surreptitious.

>*The covert operation was a success, but only a few people would ever know its significance.*

credence *(KREE-dence), noun*
Acceptance as factual; legitimacy. *Credence* is belief or plausibility.

>*His pacifist arguments lost credence when he admittedthat he had worked for a defense contractor for some years.*

credulous *(KREJ-uh-luss), adjective*
Given to acceptance or belief. A *credulous* person is one who accepts even outlandish assertions easily.

>*The swindler found a ready market for his wares in the credulous townsfolk.*

culinary *(KYOO-luh-neh-ree), adjective* ·
Pertaining to cookery or the preparation of food. A chef attends a *culinary* school.

>*His expertise in the culinary arts eventually led to a position at the city's finest restaurant.*

culminate *(KUL-mih-nate), verb*
To climax or reach a high point. Something that

culminates concludes or reaches its fulfillment.

> *The seemingly endless series of Union victories culminated in Lee's surrender at Appomatox.*

culpable *(KUL-puh-bull)*, *adjective*
Blameworthy; accountable for error or wrongdoing. Someone who is *culpable* is responsible for misdeed.

> *After Ryan was found culpable for the financial mismanagement at his firm, he was forced to resign.*

cumbersome *(KUM-ber-sum)*, *adjective*
Hard to manage; awkward in handling due to bulk, weight, or extent. Something that is troublesome and unwieldy is *cumbersome.*

> *The six-volume set is exhaustive, but rather cumbersome; I prefer the abridged version.*

cupidity *(kyoo-PID-ih-tee)*, *noun*
Greed; extreme desire for wealth. One who is obsessed with acquiring money shows *cupidity.*

> *Paul's cupidity led to much unhappiness and sorrow in later life, though his wealth was not to be denied.*

curative *(KYOOR-uh-tive)*, adjective
Curing; serving to provide a remedy. *Curative* refers to the ability to provide alleviation of an ailment.

> *The curative measures were slow but effective; Joseph eventually recovered completely.*

dalliance *(DAL-ee-unce)*, *noun*
A lighthearted undertaking; carefree spending of time. A *dalliance* is an inconsequential event. (The word often refers to an amorous flirtation or distraction).

Jean made a show of being jealous, but the truth was she understood Brian's past dalliances.

dank *(dank), adjective*
Damp and chilly. That which is unpleasantly cold and moist is *dank*.

Inside the cold, dank recesses of the cave, Fred felt suddenly and terrifyingly isolated.

debacle *(dih-BA-kull), noun*
Utter collapse or rout. A *debacle* is a complete (often ludicrous) failure. The word originally referred to collapsing sheets of river ice.

The initiative seemed promising enough, but turned out to be another of George's debacles.

debauchery *(dih-BOCH-er-ee), noun*
Licentiousness; overindulgent sexual expression. To accuse someone of *debauchery* is to say that person is intemperate and immoral with regard to indulgence in physical pleasures.

DeSade's critics claimed they had only to consult his writings for evidence of his own debauchery.

debilitate *(dih-BILL-ih-tate), verb*
To enfeeble or weaken. Something that *debilitates* a person devitalizes him and depletes his strength.

Fran's debilitating illness slowly sapped her will to live.

debonair *(deb-uh-NAIR), adjective*
Suave; sophisticated and charming. *Debonair* derives from the French for "of good lineage."

Paul's debonair manner never abandoned him, even at the most difficult moments.

decadence *(DEK-uh-dunce), noun*
Characterized by declining moral standards. *Decadence* can refer to the declining standards of a nation, a period of time, or an individual.

> *After six months on the prairie, Clyde found it difficult to return to what he saw as the decadence of city life.*

Decalogue *(DEK-uh-log), noun*
The Ten Commandments. *Decalogue* refers to the commandments given to Moses on Mount Sinai as recounted in the Bible.

> *Mr. Collins, we are dealing here with a series of administrative guidelines we may administer as we see fit--not with a Decalogue.*

decorum *(di-COR-um), noun*
Social propriety; dignified conduct. *Decorum* can also refer to a harmonious union of elements in a piece of art or literature.

> *Though the delegates were extremely frustrated at the chairman's move, they betrayed no emotion, and strict decorum was observed in the meeting hall.*

decrepit *(di-KREP-it), adjective*
Enfeebled, as by old age. *Decrepit* can refer to a weakened person, or to an object or idea that is past its prime.

> *The car's decrepit appearance was deceiving; Colin found it capable of 75 mph on the highway, and it got very good mileage.*

deduce *(di-DOOSE), verb*
To infer; to derive from evidence or assumption. *Deduce* can also mean to trace down, but the logical sense is much more widespread.

> *Holmes looked around the garden and somehow deduced that the killer was a man of middle age with*

thinning brown hair, approximately six feet tall.

deescalate *(dee-ES-kuh-late), verb*
To diminish in size, intensity, or extent. *Deescalate* is the opposite of escalate.

> *The president's decision to deescalate the war won him considerable support on the nation's college campuses.*

defamation *(def-uh-MAY-shun), noun*
False, baseless attack on a person's or group's reputation. To *defame* is to disgrace; defamation is the act of defaming.

> *After the last of the* Journal's *articles on her, Virginia decided she had put up with enough defamation and decided to sue.*

deference *(DEF-er-ence), noun*
Due respect or submission to the ideas and/or judgment of another. *Deference* is the courtesy of yielding to a (presumably higher, senior, or more authoritative) entity.

> *In deference to my family's wishes, I am not discussing this issue with the media.*

degenerate *(di-JEN-er-it), adjective and noun*
Having regressed or descended to a lower state. As a noun, *degenerate* means a person who has declined to a point of immorality or low refinement.

> *What began as an intellectually rigorous debate concluded as a degenerate shouting match.*

deja vu *(day-zhuh VOO), noun*
The experience of seeming to have seen or experienced a present event at some time in the past. *Deja vu* is French for "already seen."

> *Those who remember the format of last year's test may feel a sense of deja vu upon reviewing this year's.*

deify *(DAY-ih-fy), verb*
To elevate to the level of divinity. When something is *deified*, it is exalted or revered as godlike.

> *To promote a celebrity is one thing, to deify him quite another.*

deign *(dane), verb*
To consider (an action) appropriate or suitable to one's station or reputation; to assent or condescend to something. *Deign*, as a verb, carries a sense of haughtiness and superiority. It is often used ironically.

> *Do I understand you to say that you will not deign to answer our questions?*

delectable *(de-LEK-tuh-bull), adjective*
Highly pleasing; enjoyable (especially of a food). *Delectable* is derived from the Latin root for "delightful."

> *The Thanksgiving table was crammed with delectable dishes, but they would not be eaten that night; the news from abroad had diminished everyone's appetite.*

deleterious *(del-i-TEER-ee-us), adjective*
Harmful or injurious. *Deleterious* is a word used primarily in legal circles to give a sense of formality to the assessment of harm.

> *My client was regularly subjected to high radiation levels, hazardous compounds, and many other deleterious environmental conditions.*

delineate *(di-LIN-ee-ate), verb*
To outline; to describe the primary features of. One can *delineate* by sketching, or by using words or concepts to describe the principle points of something.

> *The rules, which had been quite vague, were now delineated clearly.*

delusion *(de-LOO-zhun)*, *noun*
An accepted (but undetected) falsehood. To delude is to deceive or mislead; a *delusion* is an instance of that act.

His delusions increased to such a point that rational discussion was impossible.

demagogue *(DEM-uh-gog)*, *noun*
An individual (usually a politician or other leader) who gains power by appealing to the emotions and passions of the people, especially by means of inflamed speech. *Demagogues* often address complicated issues by suggesting simplistic measures that appeal to public prejudice or misconception.

The senator's aides honestly believed that they had agreed to go to work for a statesman, but saw now that they were furthering the ambitions of a demagogue.

demarcate *(de-MAR-kate)*, verb
To establish the limits of. *Demarcating* is the process of setting down boundaries.

The idea of a new house had been abstract, but once Joan and Peter demarcated the land, their undertaking felt suddenly real.

dementia *(duh-MEN-chuh)*, *noun*
A mental illness characterized by loss of reason. *Dementia* is caused by neuron damage or loss within the brain.

Owing to the deceased's dementia at the time the will was signed, there was considerable legal wrangling over the estate.

demure *(di-MYOOR)*, *adjective*
Modest; affecting a reserved and shy appearance. Someone whose behavior is (outwardly, at least) sober, retiring, or sedate is *demure*.

Mr. Atkins found the Hallis twins demure, and

wondered at what they would say about him when he left.

denote *(de-NOTE), verb*
To indicate or make clear; to serve as sign or symbol for something else. To say that A *denotes* B is to say that A signifies or indicates B.

Her chills and discoloration, Dr. Smith observed, denoted severe hypothermia.

denunciation *(de-nun-see-AY-shun), noun*
The act or example of denouncing. *Denunciation* is the act of accusing another (usually in a public forum) of some misdeed.

Paul's angry denunciation of his former company shocked even his friends.

deplorable *(de-PLORE-uh-bull), adjective*
Extremely reproachful; worthy of censure. Something that is *deplorable* is wretched or grievous.

Bill's spelling was deplorable; all his friends told him it was hopeless to pursue a career as a proofreader.

depravity *(dih-PRAV-ih-tee), noun*
Corruption, moral reprehensibility. Someone who corrupts something or introduces wickedness to it commits *depravity*.

The depravity of those years is still summoned up with reverence by some of our more naive writers.

deprecate *(DEP-ri-kate), verb*
To belittle or make known one's disapproval of. To *deprecate* someone is to "cut him down" verbally.

Jean insisted that her report contained not a single deprecating word, but it was easy enough to read between the lines.

dereliction *(dare-uh-LIK-shun), noun*
Willful neglect; shirking of responsibility. *Dereliction* is the knowing failure to perform one's duty.

> *The sergeant's inaction that night led to troubling accusations of dereliction of duty.*

derision *(de-RIZH-un), noun*
Ridicule. *Derision* is formed from the verb "deride," meaning "to belittle or make light of something or someone."

> *War seems imminent; our suggestions on finding a peaceful solution to this crisis have been met with derision from the other side.*

derivation *(dare-ih-VAY-shun), noun*
Source. Also: the act or process of deriving. A thing's *derivation* is its origin or path of descent.

> *The phrase's derivation is unclear, but it may have its roots in an obscure tribal dialect of Borneo.*

desecrate *(DESS-ih-krate), verb*
To abuse the sacred character of a thing. Those who write lewd sayings on a church wall, for instance, *desecrate* the church.

> *Such profane language from our organization's current leader serves only to desecrate the memory of the founder.*

desideratum *(di-sid-uh-RAH-tum), noun*
A thing to be desired. *Desideratum* finds its plural in *desiderata*, which is also the name of a popular short writing that outlines worthy spiritual objectives.

> *He eventually accepted that her love was a fleeting desideratum, one he could learn in time to do without.*

despondency *(di-SPON-dun-see), noun*
Dejection; depression. *Despondency* is marked by a feeling that all hope is in vain.

> *It took Cloris several weeks to emerge from the despondency that accompanied her breakup.*

despotism *(DESS-po-tiz-um), noun*
Authoritarian rule. *Despotism* is a system where one dominant figure exercises complete power.

> *It was not until some years after the revolution began that the General's despotism passed into history.*

desultory *(de-SUL-to-ree), adjective*
Aimless. A person or thing lacking guidance or progressing randomly can be said to be *desultory*.

> *Unable to believe it was his last day on the job, Bill wandered through the building, desultory.*

dexterous *(DEK-ster-uss), adjective*
Skillful. *Dexterous* has its roots in the Latin for "right"--since that is the hand with which the majority of people are most skillful.

> *Byron proved a dexterous carpenter, making few errors even in his earliest days as an apprentice.*

diabolical *(die-uh-BOL-ih-kul), adjective*
Devilish, evil. Something *diabolical* is considered to be wicked or cruel.

> *The terrorists, the papers claimed, had a diabolical agenda.*

diagnostic *(die-ug-NOSS-tik), adjective*
Of or pertaining to diagnosis. Something used in evaluating a person's or thing's condition can be said to be *diagnostic* in nature.

The mechanic ran a diagnostic computer test on the car.

dialectic *(die-uh-LEK-tic), adjective and noun*

Having to do with logical arguments. (Also: *dialectical*.) As a noun, *dialectic* means the practice of arriving nearer to the truth by means of logical examination.

The dialectic thoroughness with which Paul could destroy an opponent's argument was legendary.

diatribe *(DIE-uh-tribe), noun*

Bitter denunciation. A *diatribe* is a pointed and abusive critique.

The professor had scrawled a scathing diatribe in red on the unfortunate boy's paper.

dichotomy *(die-KOT-uh-me), noun*

Division into two (contrasting) halves, pairs, or sets. A *dichotomy* is the division of mutually exclusive ideas or groups.

"There is public interest and there is private interest," said the Senator, "and reconciling that dichotomy can be a difficult job."

didactic *(die-DAK-tik), adjective*

Made or framed for the purpose of moral or ethical betterment. To say a work of art is *didactic* is to say that it forwards a clear vision of what is right and wrong, a vision the artist would like to pass on to his audience.

Simpson's early writings let the reader draw his own conclusions, but his later work is extremely didactic.

diffident *(DIFF-ih-dunt), adjective*

Unassertive and lacking a sense of self-worth. A shy, retiring person can be said to be *diffident*.

Cheryl was perhaps too diffident to work comfortably in such an outgoing office environment.

dilapidated *(di-LAP-ih-date), adjective*
To fall into disrepair. To *dilapidate* is to decay or break down.

> *The dilapidated barn swayed, heaved, and finally collapsed before Caitlyn's eyes.*

dilatory *(DIL-uh-tore-ee), adjective*
Likely to cause delay. That which proceeds at an unsatisfactorily slow rate is *dilatory*.

> *The workers' dilatory attitude lost them a large contract.*

dilettante *(DIL-uh-tont), noun*
Someone with only an amateurish or aimless interest in a subject or discipline. A man who cultivates a superficial knowledge of modern art solely to impress others, for instance, might be called a *dilettante*.

> *The cafe was once a meeting-place for struggling artists and poets of genuine talent, but by 1970 it was nothing more than a swamp of dilettantes.*

diminution *(dim-ih-NOO-shen), noun*
Reduction or decrease due to outside influence. In music, *diminution* is the repetition of a theme in notes of briefer duration than the original passage.

> *The stock fell in value by 75% in just over three hours; few issues can fully recover from such diminution.*

diplomacy *(dih-PLO-muh-see), noun*
The conduct of relations among nations. *Diplomacy* can also refer to a tact among individuals that calls to mind the great discretion and sensitivity required of diplomats.

When diplomacy fails, it is too often the young who pay the price of death on the battlefield.

discombobulate *(diss-kum-BOB-yoo-late), verb*
To confuse or throw into an awkward predicament. To say that someone is *discombobulated* is to say that he is utterly disconcerted.

The frenzied pace of eight hours on the trading floor had left me utterly discombobulated.

discomfit *(diss-KUM-fit), verb*
To cause to come into disorder. *Discomfit* can also mean "to frustrate (someone)."

Fern's household was discomfited by the sudden, unannounced arrival of her relatives.

disconcerting *(diss-kun-SERT-ing), adjective*
Ruffled; upset. That which upsets harmony or balance is *disconcerting.*

Michelle's escapades were quite disconcerting to her parents.

disdain *(diss-DANE), verb*
To treat with contempt; to dismiss haughtily. To *disdain* is to reject due to unworthiness.

Mark disdains Janet's company; he cannot forgive her lapse at last September's party.

disgruntle *(diss-GRUN-tull), verb*
To cause to become cross or discontented. To *disgruntle* is also to cause to feel cheated.

After years of mistreatment, the disgruntled employees finally decided to strike.

disingenuous *(diss-in-JEN-yoo-uss)*, *adjective*
Less than honest; unstraightforward. *Disingenuous* refers to
something scheming, crafty, or sly.

> *After receiving $6000 in repair bills over two months,*
> *Merton began to suspect that the used car dealer he had*
> *bought the car from had been disingenuous with him.*

disparage *(diss-PARE-udge)*, *verb*
To speak or write debasingly of. To *disparage* is to
communicate in such a way as to diminish another's reputation.

> *His disparaging remarks damaged both her character and*
> *her pride.*

disparate *(DISS-puh-rut)*, *adjective*
Utterly dissimilar. Two things entirely or fundamentally different
can be said to be *disparate*.

> *After inviting his mother to live on the East Coast with*
> *him, Clark wondered at how they would reconcile their*
> *disparate lifestyles.*

disparity (diss-PARE-ih-tee), noun
The condition of being inequivalent or unequal. *Disparity* is
inequality in age, measure, or extent.

> *The disparity between the two horses was obvious: one*
> *was a swaybacked old nag, the other a stunning*
> *thoroughbred.*

disport (dih-SPORT), verb
To play or frolic. To find a diversion is to *disport* oneself.

> *Jean and Michael disported themselves at the amusement*
> *park for the better part of the morning.*

disseminate (diss-SEM-ih-nate), verb
To scatter across a broad spectrum; to spread far and wide. To
disseminate is to promulgate (a message, for instance).

*In disseminating this information, Mr. Powers placed
innumerable foreign operatives at grave risk.*

dissipate *(DISS-ih-pate)*, *verb*
To dispel by means of dispersal. To *dissipate* is also to vanish
or cease.

The rain dissipated and the flood waters receded.

dissolution *(diss-so-LOO-shun)*, *noun*
The act of dissolving into fragments or parts. *Dissolution* is the
disintegration of that which comprises something.

*The union's dissolution seemed imminent, but a change
of leadership forestalled that crisis.*

dissonance *(DISS-uh-nunce)*, *noun*
A harsh or inharmonious combination, especially of sounds.
Elements of a logical argument that are in conflict can also be
said to be in *dissonance*.

*I could have no peace; the city's dissonance poured
unceasingly into my apartment.*

dissuade *(diss-SWADE)*, *noun*
To convince to take alternate action. Someone who *dissuades*
someone from doing something persuades that person to
pursue another course.

Marge dissuaded her brother from joining the army.

diurnal *(dye-UHR-nul)*, *adjective*
Occurring during the daytime. That which is not nocturnal and
occurs only while the sun is out is *diurnal*.

*Unlike other members of this species, the one we are
studying is diurnal.*

divergence *(di-VER-gence), noun*
The act or process of departing from a given course or
pattern. That which extends in separate directions from a single
point experiences a *divergence*.

>   *The divergence in our opinions begins with the question
>   of whether there can ever be a just war.*

DNA *(dee enn ay), noun*
A molecule that carries genetic information in all life forms.
The workings of *DNA* are central concerns of biology and
genetics.

>   *The fantasy film* E.T. *led us to believe that space aliens,
>   like humans, possess DNA, but it is safe to say that
>   scientists are fairly skeptical about the whole subject.*

docile *(DOSS-ul), adjective*
Easily taught. In addition, someone is *docile* if he is submissive
and easily led.

>   *Susan was docile in her younger days, but shows a real
>   independent streak now.*

dogmatic *(dog-MAT-ik), adjective*
Adhering rigidly to a principle or belief. Someone who takes a
dogmatic approach to an issue stays within ideological bounds
at all times, even when circumstances might seem to dictate
another course.

>   *The most dogmatic of the king's advisors proved to be of
>   little help during the crisis.*

domesticate *(do-MESS-ti-kate), verb*
To make accustomed to home life. To *domesticate* often carries
the sense of refining another's "uncivilized" instincts.

>   *Though she had done her best to domesticate Charles,
>   Prudence had to admit that he was still a difficult
>   marriage partner.*

domicile *(DOM-ih-sile)*, *noun*
A residence. A *domicile* is one's legal, permanent home.

> *The defendant at that time had no domicile, your honor; she was a homeless person.*

dossier *(DOSS-ee-ay)*, *noun*
A collection of documents offering detailed information on a particular individual or topic. Keeping or referring to a *dossier* on someone often carries sinister overtones of that person's espionage or subversion.

> *Marie finally obtained her dossier by means of an appeal underthe Freedom of Information Act.*

droll *(drole)*, *adjective*
Wryly amusing. Something that is strikingly odd and humorous is *droll*.

> *The little volume was filled with droll illustrations that further undermined any attempt at authoritativeness.*

dubious *(DOO-bee-uss)*, *adjective*
Tending to cause skepticism, uncertainty, or doubt. *Dubious* can also mean "reluctant to accept a particular version or account (of something.)"

> *His claim of direct descent from Richard II was regarded as dubious at best.*

dyslexia *(dis-LEKS-ee-uh)*, *noun*
Unusual trouble with spelling or reading caused by a brain condition. *Dyslexia* is rooted in an impairment in interpreting spatial relationships.

> *Judith's dyslexia frequently caused her to transpose letters in words.*

ebullience *(ih-BOLL-yunce)*, *noun*
The quality of being optimistic in speech or writing;

vivaciousness. *Ebullience* is the expression of feelings or notions in a lively, upbeat manner.

Sharon's ebullience in delivering the presentation really set her apart from the others on the team.

eccentric *(ek-SEN-trik), adjective*
Unpredictable; erratic or marked by unconventional behavior. Someone who is given to odd behavior can be considered *eccentric*.

Lionel's eccentric behavior eventually led to problems with his father.

ecclesiastical *(ih-klee-zee-ASS-ti-kul), adjective*
Pertaining to religious practices. *Ecclesiastical* refers to anything meant for or appropriate for use in a church.

The Pope's encyclical dealt not with secular issues but with ecclesiastical matters.

echelon *(ESH-uh-lon), noun*
A level of command. Literally, *echelon* pertains to military organizational structure.

Tom's proposal eventually won the approval of the company's upper echelon.

eclectic *(ek-LEK-tic), adjective*
Choosing from a variety of sources or origins. Something that offers a diverse selection of items, styles, or approaches is said to be *eclectic*.

Ryan's anthology offers selections from authors from around the world, resulting in a rather eclectic volume.

ecumenical *(ek-yoo-MEN-ih-kul), adjective*
Universal. *Ecumenical* is often used to refer to the beliefs, movements, and actions common to the various branches of Christianity worldwide.

This is not a Protestant question or a Catholic question, but a matter of ecumenical significance.

edification *(ed-ih-fih-KAY-shun), noun*

Enlightenment. To edify someone is to instruct him or share important insights with him; *edification* is the process by which this is done.

Although the author includes several supplements on ancient Egyptian construction methods for the edification of his readers, these are not directly connected with the book's central idea.

educe *(ee-DYOOCE), verb*

To draw out. *Educe* also means to reason out or establish from given facts.

Myron's attempts to educe his sister's whereabouts were futile.

effect *(ih-FEKT), verb and noun*

To accomplish or bring about (a thing). To effect a change is to cause a change to happen. *Effect* is frequently mistaken for *affect* (see *affect*). As a noun, an *effect* is a change resulting from a cause or action.

The doctors were not able to effect a cure for the disease; Ron passed away shortly after dusk on the 24th.

effeminate *(eh-FEM-uh-nit), adjective*

More reminiscent of women than men. *Effeminate* was once a positive description of female refinement; today, it is more common as a derogatory word used to question a male's masculinity. (Contrast this word with *effete*, below.)

Dean, a quiet, thoughtful boy, was sometimes labeled as effeminate by his crueler classmates.

effete *(uh-FEET), adjective*

Lacking robust vitality; sterile; without force. *Effete* originally meant exhausted from the labors of childbirth, but is rarely if ever used in that context today.

Thomas was labeled an effete snob by some, but Jane had seen him work miracles in the office through pure concentration of effort and solid teamwork.

efflorescent *(ef-flore-RES-sunt), adjective*
Blossoming. *Efflorescent* is a biological term used to describe the final development of something, but it is used by metaphor in other contexts, as well.

The poet's middle years were marked by some remarkable--and efflorescent--work of unparallelled quality.

effrontery *(ih-FRON-ter-ee), noun*
Impudent boldness. *Effrontery* is shameless audacity.

She had the effrontery to ask for a raise after three months of dreadful performance.

effulgent *(ih-FULJ-unt), adjective*
Radiant; brilliantly shining. Something that is *effulgent* shines forth resplendently.

The explosion, devastating though it was, left the night sky so effulgent that Belva could not help but marvel at the display.

egalitarian *(ih-gal-uh-TARE-ee-un), adjective*
Arising from a belief in the equality of all persons. Something is *egalitarian* if it is scrupulously fair toward all parties.

I must admit that Miles took an egalitarian approach to assigning office space.

egocentric *(ee-go-SEN-trik), adjective*
Selfish; tending toward the belief that one's own existence is all-important. An *egocentric* person places his interests above those of all others.

His was a strange and egocentric way of life that had no place for a mate.

egregious *(ih-GREE-juss), adjective*
Flagrantly incorrect or bad. An *egregious* error is one that stands out dramatically and therefore should not have been made.

Tim, an egregious liar, is the last person I would go to for reliable information.

eke *(eek), verb*
To supplement through adversity. Also: to survive or subsist by means of hard labor or strenuous effort. *Eke* (usually used with "out") is derived from the Greek for "augment."

Roger managed to eke out an existence by working two jobs.

elicit *(ih-LISS-it), verb*
To bring out. To *elicit* is to evoke or stimulate so as to yield a response. *Elicit* is occasionally confused with *illicit*, which means "improper or illegal."

Of the many responses our broadcast elicited, I like Mrs. Miller's the best.

elitism *(ih-LEE-tiz-um), noun*
Adherence to the belief that leadership is best managed by an elite (a group considered to be the highest or best class). *Elitism* often carries negative overtones of snobbery.

We have not worked so long for democracy to see it exchanged halfheartedly for elitism.

elocution *(el-oh-KYOO-shun), noun*
An individual's style of public speech. Unlike *eloquence* (see *eloquent* below), which has to do with the content of a person's speech, *elocution* refers to the manner in which speech is delivered.

The cast's elocution left a great deal to be desired.

eloquent *(EL-oh-kwent), adjective*
Fluent and persuasive in speech or expression. *Eloquent* people are convincing and pleasant to listen to.

> *Lincoln and Douglas, both eloquent debaters, knew that much more was at stake in their public meetings than a Senate seat.*

elucidate *(ee-LOO-si-date), verb*
To make clear; to explain or provide key information leading to a full understanding. Someone who *elucidates* an issue or problem throws light on it and clarifies it.

> *What is behind Frank's bizarre work habits is something only he can elucidate.*

elusive *(ee-LOO-siv), adjective*
Difficult to perceive, comprehend, or describe. An *elusive* issue or point is one that would require real work to grasp completely.

> *Our goals are easily understood; the nature of the obstacles we face is somewhat more elusive.*

emanate *(EM-uh-nate), verb*
To issue forth as from a source. To *emanate* is to flow from a point.

> *The sounds emanating from the room next door were not comforting.*

emancipate *(ee-MAN-si-pate), verb*
To liberate. That which *emancipates* frees from restraint or oppression.

> *Lincoln's decision to emancipate the slaves is considered by many to be the most significant event of the period.*

embellish *(em-BELL-ish)*, *verb*
To ornament and beautify. To *embellish* is to improve in appearance by adornment; an embellishment, then, can be a fanciful addition (or, by extension, even a convenient exaggeration of the facts).

> *Marie's gown was embellished with tiny pearls.*

embodiment *(em-BOD-ee-ment)*, *noun*
The incarnation (of a given thing or idea); the condition of being embodied. To be the *embodiment* of something is to be so imbued with it as to be its physical representation.

> *Jane was usually the embodiment of tact; her slip at the party was most uncharacteristic.*

emeritus *(ih-MARE-ih-tuss)*, *adjective*
Emeritus describes the position of one who has retired but who still holds an honorary title corresponding to the position held prior to retirement.

> *Watkins has been awarded the position of Professor Emeritus.*

eminence *(EM-ih-nunce)*, *noun*
Superiority or outstanding notability. An *eminent* person is one of great achievements or high rank. Eminence may be used as part of a formal form of address.

> *His Eminence Cardinal Powers has asked me to respond to your letter.*

emissary *(EM-ih-sare-ee)*, *noun*
An agent acting in the interests of another party. An *emissary* is one sent to undertake a mission or task as a representative.

> *The president's emissary left on a special plane from Washington; his time of return was unknown.*

empathize *(EM-puh-thize), verb*
To share another's emotions. To *empathize* with someone is to understand and identify with his situation and feelings.

> *Although I can empathize with your plight, there is very little I can do to help.*

emphatic *(em-FA-tik), adjective*
Highlighted; extremely expressive. Something that is delivered with forceful or undeniable emphasis is *emphatic*.

> *Beth was emphatic about collecting the overdue invoice.*

emulate *(EM-yoo-late), verb*
To strive to match or better by means of imitation. Someone who *emulates* another uses that person's actions as a model for future success or mastery.

> *David always felt that the key to his success was his decision to emulate his father in his professional and home life.*

encomium *(en-KO-mee-um), noun*
Warm or glowing praise; formal (usually public) tribute. An *encomium* would be given at a retirement dinner.

> *Immediately upon completing the difficult scene, the actress was hailed with a warm encomium from the film's director.*

endemic *(en-DEM-ik), adjective*
Indigenous; characteristic of a certain place, region, or populace. When something is widespread within an area--to the extent that it helps to characterize that area--we often say the thing is *endemic* to the area.

> *Poverty in the mountain region was endemic; education was almost nonexistent.*

excommunicate *(eks-kuh-MYOO-nih-kate), verb*
To banish; to revoke formally one's status as member of a group. *Excommunicate* is used primarily with regard to members of the Catholic church who are excluded from that church due to misconduct or doctrinal conflict.

> *The priest knew that he faced excommunication if he refused to resign from the legislature.*

enervate *(EN-ur-vate), verb*
To weaken. To *enervate* is to deprive of vitality, strength, or endurance.

> *The vacation's whirlwind pace actually served to enervate Madge.*

enigmatic *(en-ig-MA-tick), adjective*
Reminiscent of an enigma; puzzling or perplexing. *Enigmatic* refers to the quality of being inexplicable or ambiguous.

> *An enigmatic scrawl across the title sheet was the only clue to the work's authorship.*

en masse *(on MASS), adverb*
Together; in one body or group. *En masse* is a French term that translates loosely as "in the form of a crowd."

> *The mob moved en masse toward the Capitol.*

enmesh *(en-MESH), verb*
To involve, entangle, or implicate. Literally, *enmesh* means to catch with a mesh net; the word has acquired a broader metaphorical sense as well.

> *The judge suddenly found himself enmeshed in the ins and outs of local politics.*

enmity *(EN-mi-tee), noun*
Mutual antagonism or hatred. To show *enmity* toward a person is to harbor animosity or bitterness toward him.

> *The enmity between the feuding families only increased with the passage of time.*

ennui *(on-noo-EE), noun*
Listlessness, dissatisfaction, or boredom. *Ennui* is French for "boredom."

A sense of ennui pervaded the office during the long offseason period.

enshrine *(en-SHRINE), verb*
To cherish as though sacred; to preserve as if held within a shrine. To *enshrine* something is to memorialize it with the special reverence associated with religious ceremonies.

There is a movement to enshrine Shoeless Joe Jackson in the Baseball Hall of Fame, but I do not think him a suitable candidate.

enthrall *(en-THRALL), verb*
To hold spellbound. To *enthrall* is to captivate or mesmerize.

Garbo's performance was simply enthralling.

entity *(EN-tuh-tee), noun*
Something that exists separately. *Entity* can also refer more broadly to existence or being.

The accounting department operated as a separate entity.

enunciate *(ee-NUN-see-ate), verb*
To articulate or pronounce. To *enunciate* something is to set it forth systematically and lucidly.

The ideas he enunciated were simple, implementable, and accepted by all.

envisage *(en-VIZ-uj), verb*
To picture or conceive of. To *envisage* is also to consider or project mentally.

The group of developers envisaged an apartment complex on the waterfront property.

epicure *(EP-ih-kyoor), noun*
A connoisseur; one who cultivates refined tastes, especially in reference to food and drink. *Epicure* is derived from the name

of the Roman philosopher Epicurus, who lived betweenm 341 and 279 B.C.

> *Matt, who never seemed at all interested in gourmet dining, has suddenly become something of an epicure.*

equanimity *(ee-kwa-NIM-ih-tee)*, noun

Even-temperedness; calmness. Someone who possesses *equanimity* keeps his composure even in a difficult situation.

> *He rebutted each of the charges against him convincingly and with equanimity.*

equivocal *(ee-KWIV-uh-kul)*, adjective

Capable of varying interpretation. Also: dubious, uncertain, or suspect. To say a statement is *equivocal* is usually to cast doubt on the sincerity or truthfulness of the person making it.

> *The equivocal nature of Paul's replies caused many to wonder about his suitability for the post.*

eradicate *(ee-RAD-ih-cate)*, verb

To do away with utterly. To *eradicate* something is to wipe it out and leave no sign of it.

> *"Until we have eradicated poverty," the priest vowed, "our struggle will continue."*

erratic *(ih-RAT-ik)*, adjective

Inconsistent; lacking a set course. Something that wanders or fluctuates unpredictably can be considered *erratic*.

> *Elaine's erratic writing style irritated her superiors, who had no time to puzzle over an indecipherable and meandering memo.*

ersatz *(AIR-sats)*, noun

An unconvincing substitute. That which is not "the real thing" is *ersatz*.

> *If you think you can pass off that ersatz diamond as the real thing, you're in for a surprise.*

erudite *(AIR-yoo-dite), adjective*
Possessing extensive knowledge on a given subject; learned. An *erudite* person has received a thorough and well-rounded education.

> *Borges is nothing if not erudite; it is clear from his short stories that he is a man of immense learning.*

esoteric *(ess-oh-TARE-ik), adjective*
Comprehensible only to a particular, restricted category of people. To say something is *esoteric* is to say it lacks broad appeal.

> *The novel is likely to be enthralling to those familiar with the Revolutionary War period; others may find it esoteric.*

espouse *(ih-SPOWZ), verb*
To advocate as though one's own. *Espouse* can also mean to take in marriage.

> *Do you have any idea how complicated it would be to implement the plans you are espousing?*

estrange *(ih-STRANGE), verb*
To alienate or remove from a position or relationship. A family member who is *estranged* by others in the family is no longer regarded as part of the group.

> *Her estranged brother made many attempts to visit, but Michelle would have no part of any such plan.*

etymology *(et-ih-MOLL-uh-gee), noun*
The study of the development and history of words. A word's *etymology* is its lineage or descent.

> *I took a little Greek in school, so I think I can make an educated guess at this word's etymology.*

euphemism *(YOO-fuh-miz-um), noun*
A word or phrase that stands in place of another because it is less offensive or blunt. A *euphemism* is the "nice" way of saying something unpleasant.

> *You say these are going to be times of challenge; isn't*

that just a euphemism for times of decreased profitability?

euphony *(YOO-fuh-nee), noun*
Harmonious language or sounds. One instance of *euphony* is pleasant-sounding, musical phrasing employed in speech or writing.

> *There came a point when what mattered was not so much what the poet said, but the euphony of his language.*

evasive *(ee-VAY-siv), adjective*
Prone to hiding. Also: deliberately ambiguous in speech or response. An *evasive* answer is one that is meant to yield as little meaningful information to the questioner as possible.

> *The defense attorney found the witness hostile and evasive on the stand.*

evince *(ee-VINCE), verb*
To prove conclusively or demonstrate. To *evince* something is to show it clearly.

> *You have not evinced a single one of the claims you put forward.*

eviscerate *(ee-VIS-uh-rate), verb*
To disembowel; to remove the entrails of. *Eviscerate* is often used metaphorically to describe the process of cutting down or reducing something almost to nothing.

> *Having eviscerated the novel's key chapter, the censor was content to let the earlier exposition stand.*

evoke *(ee-VOKE), verb*
To call forth or summon. To *evoke* is also to bring back to life through appeal to memory.

> *The sight of the old mansion evoked many bittersweet memories for Charles.*

exacerbate *(ig-ZASS-ur-bate), verb*
To worsen or aggravate. To *exacerbate* something is to make it

even more unpleasant or severe.

> *You have only exacerbated the situation by lying about your activities that night.*

excoriate *(ik-SORE-ee-ate), verb*
To denounce emphatically. Literally, *excoriate* means to remove the exterior (skin) of something.

> *To be excoriated in this way is bad enough; to endure such remarks on the floor of the Senate is a sad commentary on our times.*

exculpate *(EK-skul-pate), verb*
To remove responsibility or guilt from. To *exculpate* someone is to clear his name.

> *The fact that I was convicted is immaterial; I have been fully exculpated.*

exigency *(EK-si-jen-see), noun*
Something requiring immediate action or attention; an emergency. An *exigency* is an unexpected development of some urgency.

> *The printer's failure to meet the deadline presented us with an exigency we were ill-equipped to face.*

exonerate *(ig-ZON-uh-rate), verb*
See *exculpate*.

expeditious *(ek-spuh-DISH-uss), adjective*
Speedy and efficient. That which is conducted in a brisk manner is *expeditious*.

> *Ryan came upon an expeditious means of solving the problem that had vexed the firm for so long.*

expletive *(EK-spluh-tive)*
An exclamation, interjection, or profane oath. An *expletive* is also a "filler" word that holds a grammatical position but has no independent meaning, such as the word "it" in "It is

imperative that you read this."

> *A shower of expletives descended on the umpire from the stands.*

extenuate *(ik-STEN-yoo-ate), verb*
To reduce in seriousness, external aspect, or extent. To *extenuate* is to make a fault or error less grave.

> *The trip was delayed, not because we dawdled, but because of extenuating circumstances.*

extrapolate *(ik-STRAP-uh-late), verb*
To arrive at an estimate by examining unknown values. To *extrapolate* is to make a supposition or model based on shifting or tenuous information.

> *While there were no eyewitnesses, we can extrapolate the victim's movements that night based on his past activities.*

fabulist *(FAB-yuh-list), noun*
A liar. Someone who tells outrageously untrue stories is a *fabulist*.

> *Sir Gerald, a notorious fabulist, was not consulted for an authoritative account of the crime.*

facet *(FASS-it), noun*
A component or aspect. A *facet* is also the flat smooth surface of a polished gem. To say something is multifaceted is to say it has many dimensions or components.

> *I am afraid I am unfamiliar with this facet of the case.*

facetious *(fuh-SEE-shuss), adjective*
Playful; communicated in jest. That which is frivolous or wryly humorous is *facetious*.

> *Mark was being facetious when he suggested we stay up all night.*

fait accompli *(FATE uh-com-PLEE), noun*

Something undertaken and already concluded. A *fait accompli* (from the French for "accomplished fact") is an act or event presented as beyond challenge or attempted reversal.

> *Clive simply signed the contract without consulting his superior and presented the agreement as a fait accompli.*

fallacious *(fuh-LAY-shuss), adjective*

False; containing a logical error or serious misapprehension. *Fallacious* is derived from fallacy, which means a false notion.

> *As it turned out, McCarthy's accusations against the Army were totally fallacious.*

fastidious *(fuh-STID-ee-uss), adjective*

Attentive to detail or issues of propriety; hard to please. A *fastidious* person is meticulous, exacting, and sensitive to procedure.

> *Carl, a fastidious ledger-keeper, seemed destined to do well in the accounting department.*

fatuous *(FAT-yoo-uss), adjective*

Stupid or foolish. That which is complacently idiotic is *fatuous.*

> *She made so many fatuous remarks at the party that I became disgusted and stopped apologizing for her.*

faux pas *(foe PAW), noun*

A social error. *Faux pas* is French for "false step."

> *I'm afraid that by publicly refusing to shake hands with your opponent you've done more than commit a faux pas; you may well have lost the election.*

fealty *(FEE-ul-tee), noun*

Loyalty. Literally, *fealty* describes the historical obligation of a vassal (a person granted use of land) to a lord.

> *I don't think you have any right to keep me from looking for another job; I never took an oath of fealty here, sir.*

febrile *(FEE-brul), adjective*
Feverish. That which is marked by elevated body temperature is *febrile*.

> *Due to Mother's current febrile condition, we are uneasy about her accompanying us on the trip.*

feckless *(FEK-liss), adjective*
Ineffective or feeble. A person who lacks initiative or ability in a given area could be said to be *feckless* in that area.

> *We had hoped for a well-trained and motivated consulting firm; what showed up was a pack of feckless hangers-on.*

felicity *(fih-LISS-ih-tee), noun*
Bliss; extreme happiness. *Felicity* can also refer to something that gives rise to sublime contentment.

> *Her felicity at the news that her brother had been located knew no bounds.*

feral *(FEER-uhl), adjective*
Wild and uncontrolled (said especially of animals who were once domesticated). *Feral* can also mean "natural."

> *The islands of Hawaii suffer from a severe infestation of feral pigs not native to the area.*

fervent *(FER-vunt), adjective*
Ardent and enthusiastic. Literally, *fervent* means extremely hot. A fervent desire, then, is one that is strongly held.

> *Russell's speech was characterized by fervent emotion.*

fetid *(FET-id), adjective*
Smelly. That which has an unpleasant odor is *fetid*.

> *The fetid contents of the abandoned apartment's refrigerator are best left undescribed.*

fiasco *(fee-ASS-koe), noun*
An utter and pathetic failure. *Fiasco* derives from an Italian verb meaning "to fail."

The failure of the Administration to get the housing bill through Congress is only the latest in a series of legislative fiascos.

fiat *(FEE-at), noun*
An arbitrary pronouncement or decree. To rule by *fiat* is to constantly issue orders on one's own authority, without any check or consultation.

The king issued a fiat on the question of religious worship, but the citizenry ignored it.

fidelity *(fih-DEL-ih-tee), noun*
Faithfulness to duties; observance of responsibilities. One maintains *fidelity* in marriage by honoring a vow of sexual faithfulness.

The published book's fidelity to the author's original text is suspect.

flaunt *(flont), verb*
To display (oneself or a possession) in an ostentatious way. *Flaunt* is often confused with *flout* (see *flout* below), but the words have completely different meanings.

Mr. Miller's habit of wearing many jewelled rings is one of the many ways he has found to flaunt his wealth.

flout *(flowt), verb*
To brazenly or openly break a law, regulation, or tradition. *Flout* is often confused with *flaunt* (see *flaunt* above), but the words have completely different meanings.

To begin the baseball game without singing the national anthem would be to flout a tradition of more than a century.

fledgling *(FLEJ-ling), adjective and noun*
Young or inexperienced. Literally, a *fledgling* is a young bird that has only recently gained the power of flight.

The fledgling reporter had little respect around the newsroom.

flim-flam *(FLIM-flam), noun and adjective*
A swindle. A *flim-flam* operation is a scam or confidence game.

> *Vern may call himself an entrepreneur; he appears to me to be nothing more than a flim-flam artist.*

flippant *(FLIP-punt), adjective*
Showing an inappropriate disregard for decorum; disrespectful. A person who is *flippant* is given to shallow, tactless patter.

> *Her flippant attitude toward her superiors won her no points on the job.*

flux *(fluks), noun*
Ongoing flow. *Flux* can also refer to unceasing change.

> *The organization's plans were in a state of constant flux.*

foible *(FOI-bull), noun*
Fault or character flaw. To say a person has a *foible* is to say he exhibits a flaw or failing that is comparatively insignificant.

> *The tendency to remember only the pleasant occurences in our past is a common human foible.*

foist *(foist), verb*
To pawn off (something undesirable). To *foist* something on someone is to assign it or pass it along to him despite his wishes.

> *This project was foisted on us because everyone believed it was impossible, and because we were considered the worst department in the organization.*

fop *(fop), noun*
A dandy. An extravagant (male) person who is uncommonly vain or pretentious is a *fop*.

> *I was cornered by Charles, the biggest fop on campus, who subjected me to a lecture about how wonderfully he was dressed .*

foray *(FORE-ay), noun*
An initial try. Originally, a *foray* was a sudden military advance.

Elizabeth's foray into the world of publishing was not without disheartening moments.

formidable *(FOR-mih-duh-bull), adjective*
Capable of inspiring fear or respect. Something that is *formidable* is challenging or difficult to overcome.

> *Alfred faced a formidable opponent; he knew he had to plan carefully.*

fortuitous *(fore-TOO-ih-tuss), adjective*
Accidental; lucky or fortunate. A *fortuitous* event is one that comes as a pleasant surprise.

> *After years of trial and error, Dr. Powers made a fortuitous discovery when he mistakenly combined two chemical compounds.*

fractious *(FRAK-shuss), adjective*
Unruly; likely to cause disturbance or trouble. A *fractious* person is quarrelsome and difficult.

> *Michael's fractious nature made him an unsuitable candidate for a career in customer service.*

fratricide *(FRAT-rih-side), noun*
The act of killing a brother. *Fratricide* refers to the murder of a male sibling; the word for killing a sister is *sororicide*.

> *It is only when Hamlet is told of the king's fratricide that a tragic chain of events is initated.*

frivolity *(frih-VOL-ih-tee), noun*
Unworthy of serious note; insubstantial. To engage in *frivolity* is to behave in a lighthearted or even ludicrous way.

> *We have no time for frivolity; tomorrow morning, the manager is coming.*

fruition *(froo-ISH-un), noun*
That which has arisen from development, possession, use, or effort. The achievement of something desired or labored for is

the *fruition* of that deed.

> *The novel was, in a sense, the fruition of a lifetime of work for Melville.*

fulminate *(FUL-mih-nate), verb*
To explode. Also: to denounce loudly or forcefully. Someone who *fulminates* thunders forth or issues a dramatic attack.

> *He fulminated against the bill on the floor of the Senate, but he knew he did not have the votes to defeat it.*

funereal *(fyoo-NIR-ee-uhl), adjective*
Reminiscent of a funeral. That which is dark, brooding, and mournful is *funereal*.

> *The funereal tone of the meeting was not at all what we had in mind to raise morale.*

furtive *(FUR-tiv), adjective*
Stealthy. That which is surreptitious or sly is *furtive*.

> *Marie's furtive designs were soon detected and exposed.*

futility *(fyoo-TILL-ih-tee), noun*
That which is characterized by uselessness. Something that is impractical or vainly undertaken shows *futility*.

> *The futility of attempting to reason with Paula could no longer be denied; Michael gave up trying.*

gainsay *(GANE-say), verb*
To declare false. To *gainsay* is to oppose or contradict.

> *The principles of the Bill of Rights, Mr. Secretary, will admit no gainsaying.*

gallantry *(GAL-un-tree), noun*
Something displaying dashing bravery or chivalry. *Gallantry* pertains to an air of courage and nobility.

> *His gallantry and sophistication will do little to solve*

this problem; what is needed is cold cash.

galvanize *(GAL-vuh-nize), verb*
To arouse or summon to action. Literally, *galvanization* is the process whereby something is stimulated by means of electric current.

The letter had a galvanizing effect on Madge.

gamut *(GAM-ut), noun*
The full range or extent. *Gamut* also refers to the entire series of standard musical notes.

His house featured an entertainment center whose components ran the gamut of state-of-the-art equipment.

gargantuan *(gar-GAN-choo-un)*
Enormous. *Gargantuan* derives from a the name of a fictional king (Gargantua) famous for his massive appetite.

The gargantuan scale of the budget deficit caught both Congress and the financial markets by surprise.

garner *(GAR-nur), verb*
To amass, gather, or accumulate. To *garner* something is to acquire it over a period.

William garnered much praise for his writing but little cash.

garrulity *(guh-ROO-lih-tee), noun*
Talkativeness. *Garrulity* refers to one who is overly or habitually given to talking.

If Michael's insight only matched his garrulity, he would be quite popular.

gauche *(gohsh), adjective*
Tactless; lacking in social refinement. A socially inappropriate remark or action could be considered *gauche*.

David's constant praise of his first wife was considered gauche by his new mother-in-law.

gaudy *(GAHW-dee), adjective*
Showy; tasteless. Something that bespeaks tackiness or excessive ornamentation is *gaudy*.

For some reason, Cheryl always adorns herself with the gaudiest jewelry imaginable.

gauntlet *(GONT-let), noun*
A challenge. To "throw down the *gauntlet*," in medieval times, was to issue a challenge to a duel.

This deadline is not simply a goal for this department; it is a gauntlet that has been thrown before us.

genial *(JEEN-yul), adjective*
Kindly or pleasant in disposition. A *genial* attitude is one of warmth and openness.

Although we expected to confront the enemy in full force, we encountered only genial townsfolk.

genteel *(jen-TEEL), adjective*
Refined; conveying a sense of high style and/or respectability. *Genteel* is often meant to imply a sense of social superiority, as well.

Tom's vulgar remarks were not appreciated by his genteel dining companions.

gentry *(JEN-tree), noun*
Those claiming high birth. In England, *gentry* refers to the class immediately below the nobility.

The fact that the gentry would benefit most from victory was taken by many of the soldiers to mean that they were fighting a rich man's war.

gestation *(jes-TAY-shun), noun*
Inception and creation. The period of *gestation* among humans,

for instance, would be the nine months spent within the womb. Concepts and ideas are also said to have gestation.

> *The ad campaign's gestation was fraught with conflict, but the end result was well worth all the quarrelling.*

gesticulate *(jes-TICK-yoo-late), verb*
To employ gestures, especially in place of speech. *Gesticulate* usually implies more animation and excitement than the simpler gesture.

> *Unable to speak French, Michael was forced to gesticulate to try to make himself understood.*

globular *(GLOB-yoo-lar), adjective*
Spherically shaped. *Globular* means, primarily, "in the shape of a globe." The best word for " of worldwide interest or applicability" is global.

> *Several globular lampheads illuminated the room.*

Gnostic *(NOSS-tik), adjective*
Pertaining to or reminiscent of certain early Christian sects (known as Gnostics) who valued personal knowledge and inquiry as supreme religious values transcending physical experience. *Gnostic* also can mean "pertaining to knowldedge," especially in the context of spirituality. It is not normally used as the opposite of agnostic.

> *The ancient Gnostic gospels, while not part of my formal church teaching, nevertheless made for illuminating reading.*

goad *(goad), verb*
To stimulate, urge, or prod, especially toward a given action. Originally, a *goad* was a pointed stick used to prod animals.

> *Brian decided not to write his name on the wall, despite his friends' attempts to goad him into doing so.*

gormandize *(GORE-mun-dize), verb*
To eat in a greedy, ravenous manner. Someone who *gormandizes* eats to satisfy a voracious appetite. Someone who

does this is known as a gormand (or gourmand); this is very different from gourmet, which describes someone who cultivates refined tastes for food of the finest quantity.

> *Tom's tendency to gormandize eventually made him an unwelcome dinner guest.*

gradation *(gra-DAY-shun), noun*
A progression by state or degree. To progress in *gradation* is to move ahead in measured, distinct stages.

> *The portrait's haunting effect may be due to Singer's extremely subtle gradations of color.*

graft *(graft), noun*
The unscrupulous use of rank or formal post for personal gain. Corrupt businesspersons or politicians who profit personally in an illicit way because of their official standing could be accused of *graft*.

> *The game had been sold out for months, and the mayor's easy acquisition of choice tickets led to whisperings of graft in the administration.*

grandeur *(GRAN-jur), noun*
The quality of being grand; extravagance in scale or appearance. *Grandeur* refers to magnificence.

> *The Emerald City's grandeur exceeded anything Dorothy had ever seen.*

grandiloquence *(gran-DIL-uh-kwence), noun*
Pompous speech or expression; bombast. *Grandiloquence* refers to an attitude of haughtiness, especially in one's means of communication.

> *I may not always employ the grandiloquence my opponent does, but I believe I have a commonsense solution to the problem he has just outlined.*

grandiose (GRAN-dee-oce), adjective

Pompous. Someone whose pretentions or ambitions exceed his abilities, sensitivities, or means could be considered *grandiose.*

His grandiose scheme for career advancement simply will not pan out.

gratuitous (gruh-TOO-ih-tuss), adjective

Unnecessary. Also: given or granted without recompense or charge. Something that is *gratuitous* is excessive, out of place, or unnecessary.

His gratuitous attacks on the popular governor only weakened his standing among voters.

gregarious (gri-GARE-ee-uss), adjective

Outgoing, cordial, or friendly. *Gregarious* people enjoy the company of others.

Many would have been put off by such a reception, but Bill was unusually gregarious; he made many friends that night.

grimace (GRIM-uss)

A facial expression showing disgust or discomfort. A *grimace* is a sharp facial contortion indicating pain, dissatisfaction, or disgust.

Billy grimaced at the thought of eating his vegetables.

grope (groap), verb

To reach about blindly. *Grope* can also be used figuratively to describe someone who acts in uncertainty of purpose.

He groped for the right words, but could not manage to come up with an acceptable explanation.

grovel (GROV-ul), verb

To lie prostrate, especially when done as a sign of humility. Another meaning of *grovel* is to give oneself over completely to subservience.

To see his sister reduced to groveling for approval in this way was almost too much for Ryan to take.

guile *(gile), noun*
Cunning; treacherous deceit. Someone who exercises *guile* is insidious and misleading.

In laying the groundwork for embezzlement on such a large scale, Donald showed considerable guile and no small amount of daring.

hackneyed *(HAK-need), adjective*
Rendered less significant by common use. Literally, a *hackney* is a horse suited for routine riding or driving (and not a prime racehorse).

The primitive construction and reliance on hackneyed expressions make it perfectly clear: this is not the work of Shakespeare.

haiku *(HIE-koo), noun*
A Japanese form of poetry. A *haiku* has three lines of five, seven, and five syllables, and often evokes images from nature.

Dean even tried his hand at poetry, composing several pleasant haikus for the newsletter.

halcyon *(HAL-see-on), adjective and noun*
Tranquil. Also: prosperous, carefree. A *halcyon* is a mythical bird, identified with the Kingfisher, that could supposedly calm ocean storms.

The company's halcyon years were behind it; all was in chaos now.

hallow *(HAL-low), verb*
To establish as holy. To *hallow* can also be to extend the highest possible honor toward something.

This ancient burial ground, which is hallowed ground to many Native Americans, attracts a few too many tourists for my tastes.

haphazard *(hap-HAZ-urd)*, *adjective*
Irregular; governed by chance. Something that is done in a *haphazard* manner is not guided by a system or regular method.

> *After a few haphazard guesses at the box's contents, Steve gave up.*

hapless *(HAP-liss)*, *adjective*
Luckless, unfortunate. A *hapless* person is unlucky.

> *Oliver presented a rather hapless figure during his first few days on the job, but he soon mastered his new responsibilities.*

harangue *(huh-RANG)*, *noun*
A scolding, especially a lengthy one delivered in a public setting. *Harangue* can also be used as a verb.

> *Castro's harangue neither addressed the facts nor presented any promise of a solution to the crisis.*

harbinger *(HAR-bin-jur)*, *noun*
A forerunner. A *harbinger* foreshadows a future event or trend.

> *These figures are a harbinger of hard times to come.*

hardtack *(HARD-tak)*, *noun*
A hard biscuit once common in the rations of sailors and soldiers. *Hardtack* did not spoil--a major logistical benefit.

> *By the end of the war, the Union soldiers were thoroughly sick of the hardtack and vegetable soup that had been the mainstay of their diet.*

haute couture *(OAT kyoo-CHOOR)*, *noun*
High fashion. *Haute couture* is the most stylish and influential way of designing clothes at a given time. (*Haute couture* also refers to articles of clothing currently considered of the highest style.)

> *Unfamiliar with the ways of* haute couture, *Wendell*

decided to pass up the fashion show.

haute cuisine *(OAT kwi-ZEEN)*, *noun*
Gourmet preparation of food. *Haute cuisine* can also refer to the preparation of meals as an art form.

> *Glenn knows more than we do about haute cuisine; let's let him pick the restaurant tonight.*

hegemony *(he-JEM-uh-nee)*, *noun*
Predominant influence, especially in reference to the affairs of nations. To say one nation practices *hegemony* over another is to suggest that it exercises undue influence over conduct, mores, or administration within that nation.

> *Our foe's hegemony will not stop with his control of smaller nations; his aim is world domination.*

heinous *(HAY-nuss)*, *adjective*
Evil; reprehensible. To say something is *heinous* is to say that it far exceeds the bounds of morality.

> *Because of the heinous nature of this crime, I am forced to pass a stern sentence.*

herbicide *(URB-ih-syde)*, *noun*
A chemical that kills plants. *Herbicide* refers especially to that which eradicates weeds.

> *Although originally described as a comparatively harmless herbicide, Agent Orange was (as thousands of soldiers learned much later) anything but.*

herculean *(hur-kyuh-LEE-un)*, *adjective*
Strong and powerful; reminiscent of the god Hercules in vitality. In addition, *herculean* can mean daunting or formidable--so difficult as to require the strength of Hercules.

> *Robert made a herculean effort to complete the project before midnight.*

heretic *(HARE-uh-tic)*, *noun*
A person who professes belief in a dogma or system of belief (especially a religion), but differs with a tenet of that system.

Heretic is often used more loosely to describe a member of group or organization who airs opinions that conflict with established principles or routines.

> *His stand against the Agency's involvement in Guatemala led someto brand Clint a heretic.*

heterogeneous *(het-er-uh-JEEN-ee-us), adjective*

Different. *Heterogeneous* means consisting of utterly dissimilar parts or styles.

> *Marie invited a heterogeneous group: poets, potters, mechanics, bureaucrats, and who knows who else.*

hiatus *(hie-AY-tuss), noun*

An interruption or break. A *hiatus* is an intermission or break in continuity.

> *After a long hiatus from the stage, Peter auditioned for a role in A Midsummer Night's Dream.*

hierarchy *(HIE-uh-rar-kee), noun*

A system (of people, concepts, groups, etc.) in which there is a ranking of entities one above another. A *hierarchy* often refers to a formal chain of command.

> *The famous psychologist Abraham Maslow has established a hierarchy of human needs.*

holistic *(ho-LISS-tik), adjective*

Emphasizing wholeness and/or the cooperation of the constituent members of a thing. *Holistic* is often used to describe medical or healing practices that emphasize an organism's totality, rather than focasing exclusively on one symptom or illness.

> *Fenwick takes a holistic approach to problem-solving that has drawn much positive attention.*

homage *(HOM-ij), noun*

Display of special respect or honor. To pay *homage* to someone is to act in a way that shows high reverence or alleigance.

> *The family made the long auto trip primarily to pay*

homage to their dying uncle.

hominid *(HOM-ih-nid), noun*
A member of the animal family to which humans belong. *Hominids* are humans and their ancestors.

> *The first ten minutes of the film depict the first use of tools by a group of ancient African hominids.*

homonym *(HOM-uh-nim), noun*
A word that sounds the same as another word. "To" and "two' are *homonyms*.

> *I think in this sentence you have confused the word "real" with its homonym "reel."*

hotspur *(HOT-spur), noun*
A quick-tempered, impulsive person. *Hotspur* is the name of a fiery character in Shakespeare's play *Henry IV, Part One*.

> *Ed was a real hotspur around the office; he was likely to dominate a meeting with rash decrees and sudden denuciations of plans he did not like.*

hubris *(HYOO-briss), noun*
Excessive pride. *Hubris* can refer to the "fatal flaw" of ancient Greek drama, or (more generally) to any disproportionate pride or self-love.

> *Colin may have begun as a pleasant and unassuming clerk, but by the time he took over the company in 1987 he showed signs of the hubris that would accompany his downfall.*

hyperthermia *(hie-pur-THUR-mee-uh), noun*
Extreme increase of body heat. *Hyperthermia* derives from the Greek roots "hyper" and "thermia," meaning "above" and "heat," respectively. (Compare with *hypothermia*.)

> *The reading is 108 degrees; we are dealing not with a simple fever, but with severe hyperthermia.*

hyperbole *(hie-PUR-buh-lee) noun*
Extravagant overstatement. To exaggerate something for the

purpose of effect is to use *hyperbole*.

> *I think you can safely regard his promise to eat his hat if proven wrong as hyperbole.*

hyperopia *(hi-pe-ROH-pee-uh), noun*
Farsightedness. Those who see distant things more clearly than those that are near experience *hyperopia*.

> *Although Fran's hyperopia could have been corrected easily, she insisted on reading without glasses or contact lenses.*

hypothermia *(hie-po-THER-mee-uh), noun*
Extreme loss of body heat. *Hypothermia* derives from the Greek roots "hypo" and "thermia," meaning "below" and "heat," respectively. (Compare with *hyperthermia*.)

> *After seven hours in the freezing water, the victims had already succumbed to the effects of hypothermia.*

iconoclastic *(eye-kon-uh-KLASS-tik), adjective*
Given to attacking cherished institutions or beliefs. Taken most literally, *iconoclastic* describes a person who defaces or destroys holy images or icons.

> *Shaw's iconoclastic approach to issues of social class won him many enemies.*

ignoble *(ig-NO-bull), adjective*
Dishonorable in nature. In contrast with *ignominious* (see below), *ignoble* carries the sense of baseness or lowness.

> *Peter's ignoble aims were well known to all in the room.*

ignominious *(ig-no-MIN-ee-uss), adjective*
Shameful or disgraceful. *Ignominious* is generally used to describe public humiliation or failure.

> *Tyrone's ignominious defeat in court persuaded him to settle his other lawsuits against the company.*

illicit (ih-LISS-it), *adjective*
Illegal or morally unjustifiable. *Illicit* refers to something not sanctioned by custom or law.

> *We all know now that the money was acquired through illicit means, don't we?*

imbibe *(im-BIBE), verb*
To drink. *Imbibe* is generally used to describe the drinking of alcoholic beverages, though it can also carry the meaning "to take in (an idea)."

> *Donald once had a drinking problem, but now he no longer imbibes.*

imbroglio *(im-BROA-lee-o), noun*
An entanglement or complicated misunderstanding. *Imbroglio* refers to a delicate situation from which it is difficult to extricate oneself.

> *The recent imbroglio over conflict-of-interest violations has not improved the Mayor's standing with voters.*

imbue *(im-BYOO), verb*
To saturate or flow throughout by absorption. *Imbue* is often used metaphorically to describe the transmission of an idea, feeling, or emotion.

> *Bert's philosophy was imbued with the ideas of John Stuart Mill.*

immaculate *(im-MAK-yoo-lut), adjective*
Spotless; utterly free from fault, blemish, or stain. Something that is *immaculate* is impeccably clean.

> *After the boys had finished the cleanup job, the garage looked immaculate.*

immolate *(IM-uh-late), verb*
To kill as if as a sacrifice, especially by fire. *Immolate* derives from a Latin word that pertained to sacrificial meals.

> *The monk's dramatic act of self-immolation made headlines around the world.*

impalpable *(im-PAL-puh-bull), adjective*
Impossible to perceive through use of the sense of touch.
Impalpable also refers to anything extremely difficult to perceive
or interpret.

> *The prosecution has tried to connect my client with the*
> *murderer, but all the connections they have put forward*
> *have been impalpable ones.*

imparity *(im-PARE-uh-tee), noun*
Inequality; disparity. Things that are unequal in scope or extent
possess *imparity*.

> *The treaty will rectify the serious imparity that now*
> *exists in weapons systems.*

impasse *(IM-pass), noun*
A situation that seems to offer no solution or escape. To reach
an *impasse* is to come to a point of stalemate. Literally, an
impasse is a dead-end street or passage.

> *Tom realized that his relationship with Betty had come*
> *to an impasse; divorce was now on her mind, and he*
> *knew it.*

impeccable *(im-PECK-uh-bull), adjective*
Flawless; virtually perfect. *Impeccable* is derived from the Latin
roots for "without sin."

> *Roger, a man of impeccable taste in clothes, was wearing*
> *a particularly striking suit.*

imperative *(im-PAIR-uh-tiv), adjective and noun*
Essential, obligatory, or mandatory. As a noun, an *imperative* is
a command or an essential objective. *Imperative* also has a
grammatical sense referring to verbs that command or exhort.
(For instance, in the sentence "Sit, Rex!" the word *sit* is in the
imperative.)

> *It is imperative that the soldiers evacuate as soon as*
> *possible.*

imperceptible *(im-pur-SEP-tuh-bull), adjective*
So subtle as to be unnoticeable. *Imperceptible* refers to that
which is so gradual or unnoticeable it is virtually impossible

to perceive.

> *The distinctions you draw in this paragraph are imperceptible to the average reader.*

imperious *(im-PEER-ee-us)*, *adjective*
Haughty. Also: urgent. *Imperious* is usually meant to convey a sense of dictatorial arrogance.

> *Mrs. Banks rushed around the kitchen, issuing a series of imperious commands to the cook.*

impertinent *(im-PURR-tih-nent)*, *adjective*
Rude; brash. Something that is improper or beyond established bounds is *impertinent*.

> *What an impertinent thing to say!*

impervious *(im-PURR-vee-us)*, *adjective*
Impenetrable. Also: impossible to alter or affect. *Impervious* usually means incapable of being changed from a given course.

> *We tried to dissuade Millicent from sending the children to Montana, but she was impervious.*

impetuous *(im-PET-you-us)*, *adjective*
Impulsive. That which is driven by sudden force or emotion is *impetuous*.

> *Dirk's impetuous remark may well cost him his job.*

implicit *(im-PLISS-it)*, *adjective*
Implied or understood, though not expressed directly. An *implicit* understanding is one that two parties abide by but do not set out in specific language.

> *There was an implicit agreement between the two not to bring up the subject of Michael's first wife.*

implore *(im-PLORE)*, *verb*
To beseech or beg for fervently. To *implore* is to plead urgently.

> *She implored him to attend the party.*

importunate *(im-PORE-chuh-nit)*, *adjective*
Demanding or impatient in issuing repeated requests. An *importunate* person makes many annoying entreaties.

> *Two-year-olds, though lovable, can be importunate; Wesley seemed unprepared for this.*

impregnable *(im-PREG-nuh-bull)*, *adjective*
Stubbornly resistant. Something that is *impregnable* is unshakeable and/or unconquerable.

> *The town proved impregnable, despite the army's repeated assaults.*

impropriety *(im-pruh-PRY-ih-tee)*, *noun*
Incorrectness. An *impropriety* is a misdeed or crossing of established social mores.

> *Beverly's minor impropriety at the dinner table was overlooked; the conversation turned quickly to other topics.*

impugn *(im-PYOON)*, *verb*
To brand as false in argument or discourse. *Impugn* usually implies an open attack or challenge upon another's honesty or motives.

> *Are you attempting to impugn my husband's version of the attack?*

impunity *(im-PYOO-nih-tee)*, *noun*
Freedom from punishment or penalty. *Impunity* is sometimes confused with *impugn* (above), especially in its spelling.

> *We cannot let such an act of naked aggression stand with impunity.*

inadvertent *(in-ad-VER-tnt)*, *adjective*
Unintentional. *Inadvertent* can also refer to carelessness or inattention.

> *His inadvertent slight cast a cloud of gloom over the proceedings.*

inane *(in-ANE), adjective*
Pointless or lacking in substance. Something that is *inane* is vacuous.

Among other inane suggestions, Jeff proposed painting the lunchroom in a polka-dot pattern.

incarnate *(in-KAR-nut), adjective*
Embodied. Something that takes the bodily or physical form (especially human form) of "X" is said to be "X *incarnate*."

Sarah is not simply quiet; she is tranquility incarnate.

inception *(in-SEP-shun), noun*
Beginning. *Inception* refers to the generation of an idea or organism, from its initial developmental stages onward.

The car was riddled with design flaws, most dating back to the auto's inception in 1972.

incessant *(in-SESS-unt), adjective*
Continuous. *Incessant* derives from the Latin roots for "without end."

His incessant questions can become quite annoying.

inchoate *(in-KO-ate), adjective*
Incomplete. *Inchoate* refers to something still in early development.

The concept, which Glenn readily admitted was inchoate, showed promise despite its flaws.

incipient *(in-SIP-ee-unt), adjective*
At an early stage. *Incipient* is an adjective from the same root as the noun *inception*.

There is an incipient problem in this area that must be resolved quickly and decisively.

incisive *(in-SYE-siv), adjective*
Penetrating or sharp in analysis, observation, etc. *Incisive* derives from the Latin root for "cutting."

An incisive Times *review of the play notes that the dialogue is similar in many places to passages from the works of Proust.*

inclement *(in-CLEM-unt), adjective*

Harsh. *Inclement* is often used to refer to the condition of the weather.

The unexpected inclement weather ruined our vacation.

incognito *(in-cog-NEE-to), adjective*

Hidden or unknown. To intentionally change appearance in such a way as to make one's real identity unknown is to go *incognito*.

The novelist wore sunglasses in hopes of remaining incognito at restaurants, but he was still pestered by autograph hounds.

incorporeal *(in-core-PORE-ee-al), adjective*

Lacking form. *Incorporeal* derives from the Latin roots meaning "without the body."

The moanings and low rumblings in the old house suggested incorporeal visitors to Kate.

incorrigible *(in-KORE-ij-uh-bul), adjective*

(Apparently) incapable of being reformed. *Incorrigible* is often used in a lighthearted, ironic sense.

Young Pete was an incorrigible boy, forever getting into scrapes and causing mischief.

inculcate *(IN-kul-kate), verb*

To instill (learning) by means of repetition or instruction. To *inculcate* is to impress an idea upon someone with urging or earnest example.

Rachel tried to inculcate the virtue of thrift in her daughter.

inculpate *(in-KUL-pate), verb*

To incriminate. To blame for a wrongdoing is to *inculpate*.

Myra's frequent visits to the scene of the crime, in Sarah's view, inculpated her as the guilty party.

indefatigable *(in-di-FAT-ih-guh-bul), adjective*
Tireless. Someone who possesses unyielding stamina is *indefatigable*.

> *Betty, an indefatigable runner, never seemed to slow her pace.*

indelible *(in-DELL-ih-bul), adjective*
Unremovable. An *indelible* mark is one that is not easily erased or cleansed away.

> *Carl leaves an indelible impression on those he meets.*

indemnify *(in-DEM-nih-fy), verb*
To protect from or provide compensation for damages. To *indemnify* is to shield against the loss, destruction, or damage of something.

> *This policy indemnifies my house against fire, flood, and burglary.*

indolent *(IN-duh-lnt), adjective*
Lazy, as a way of life. Someone who is *indolent* is inactive and unlikely to exert himself.

> *Peter, an indolent young man, spent his young days gazing out the window daydreaming.*

inebriated *(in-EE-bree-ate-ud), adjective*
Intoxicated. Someone who is *inebriated* is drunk.

> *The two men at the bar became steadily more inebriated as the night wore on.*

ineffable *(in-EFF-uh-bull), adjective*
Beyond the capacity of expression. Also: forbidden as a subject of conversation. Something that is *ineffable* is indescribable or unspeakable.

> *Carlton presented new acquaintances with a certain ineffable charm that lingered long after one's first*

meeting with him.

ineluctable *(in-ee-LUK-tuh-bull), adjective*
Unavoidable; impossible to overcome. Something that is inevitable is *ineluctable*.

> *Oedipus' fate, we must remember, is ineluctable; no amount of struggling will free him from it.*

inept *(in-EPT), adjective*
Inappropriate. Someone who lacks judgment, discretion, or ability can be said to be *inept*.

> *Williams, an inept craftsman, soon found that his goods would never fetch top dollar.*

inertia *(in-UR-shuh), noun*
Sluggishness; the quality of being inert. In physics, *inertia* is the tendency of an object to resist change (acceleration or change in direction, for instance) unless acted on by an outside force.

> *It is not a lack of opportunity that has hampered you, Jackson, but simple inertia.*

inexorable *(in-EK-sur-uh-bul), adjective*
Unyielding. Something that is stubborn or unwavering is *inexorable*.

> *"The inexorable advance of our troops," the Union general said happily, "will complicate things for Mr. Davis."*

inexplicable *(in-eks-PLIK-uh-bul), adjective*
Defying explanation or interpretation. That which is hard to communicate is *inexplicable*.

> *My opponent's failure to file income tax returns is inexplicable.*

infallible *(in-FAL-uh-bul), adjective*
Incapable of making a mistake. Something that is regarded as beyond error might be said to be *infallible*.

You have no need to worry about the security of this mission, gentlemen; the HAL 9000 computer is infallible.

infer *(in-FUR), verb*
To gather by reasoning. To *infer* is not the same as to imply, which means "to leave the suggestion that."

I think we can infer here that the author is using the character as a mouthpiece of sorts to air her own concerns.

infernal *(in-FER-nul), adjective*
Fiendish; devilish. *Infernal* means, literally, "of or pertaining to hell." It is often used as a mild expletive.

This infernal copier keeps breaking down!

infidel *(IN-fih-del), noun*
A person who does not accede to a particular set of religious beliefs. An *infidel* is an unbeliever; the word is often used metaphorically to refer to those who are unpersuaded of the wisdom and/or righteousness of a position or principle.

Because he failed to express the proper enthusiasm for Riley's campaign proposal, Wilson was regarded as something of an infidel.

infidelity *(in-fi-DEL-ih-tee) noun*
The quality or act of having been untrue or inconsistent with an (often implied) standard. *Infidelity* is often used to describe extramarital affairs.

Although Gwen suspected her husband of infidelity, she had not come across any tangible proof.

infrastructure *(IN-fruh-struk-chur), noun*
Foundation; underlying base. An *infrastructure* is the collection of essential primary components of a system, organization, or structure.

The architect guessed that the infrastructure had probably begun to erode at the turn of the century; the building was now beyond repair.

ingrate *(IN-grate), noun*
An ungrateful person. A person who does not show the proper respect or gratitude toward someone who has provided help might be called an *ingrate*.

> *He lived with us for six months, but that ingrate Ralph hasn't even written in over two years.*

inherent *(in-HARE-unt), adjective*
Intrinsic; necessary. An important or essential part of something can be said to be *inherent*.

> *Dwayne's inherent reluctance to entrust newcomers with tasks of any significance was a major problem for the company.*

inimical *(in-IM-ih-kul), adjective*
Harmful; injurious. Something that possesses a dangerous or hostile character can be said to be *inimical*.

> *I'm afraid this work environment is inimical to creative thinking.*

iniquity *(ih-NIK-wih-tee), noun*
Injustice or immoral action. *Iniquity* derives from the Latin for "unfairness."

> *The many iniquities suffered by American Indians at the hands of government authorities is only now being widely acknowledged.*

innate *(ih-NATE), adjective*
Possessed at birth. Something that is inborn or central to a person or thing can be said to be *innate*.

> *Sol's innate sense for what will make a good plan has served him well since he was a small boy.*

innocuous *(ih-NOK-yoo-us), adjective*
Harmless. Also: lacking conflict or drama. Something is *innocuous* if it shows minimal significance, interest, or prominence.

> *The editor rejected my first news story, which I found fascinating but he considered innocuous.*

inoculate *(ih-NOK-yoo-late), verb*
To facilitate the buildup of resistance to a disease by introducing a minuscule sample of its virus into the body. *Inoculate* derives from the Latin for "to graft onto."

> *Marie, normally frightened of injections, summoned up all her courage when it came time for the doctor to inoculate her against smallpox.*

inroad *(IN-road), noun*
An opening or entry (said especially of a new idea, campaign, or undertaking). *Inroad* originally referred to a military maneuver during invasion.

> *The new brand of cookies was still unknown in the South, although it had made significant inroads in the Midwest.*

inscrutable *(in-SKROO-tuh-bul), adjective*
Dense or difficult to fathom; resisting of scrutiny. Something that is hard to decipher could be called *inscrutable*.

> *Tom's inscrutable smile made many in the room uneasy.*

insidious *(in-SID-ee-uss), adjective*
Enticing yet harmful. Something that spreads or is widely accepted despite its (perhaps subtle) harmful nature could be said to be *insidious*.

> *Kudzu, an attractive but insidious Southern weed, may infiltrate the New England countryside before too long.*

insipid *(in-SIP-d), adjective*
Lacking in vigor; dull. *Insipid* (usually applied to bland ideas, personalities, or works of art) derives from the Latin for "without taste."

> *In Frank's opinion, the novel's plot was insipid and left much to be desired.*

insolent *(IN-suh-lnt), adjective*
Rude and arrogant. That which is insulting or disrespectful (especially speech) could be considered *insolent*.

> *Her insolent retorts to Joan's well-intentioned queries*

stunned the dinner party.

insubordinate *(in-sub-BOR-dn-it), adjective*
Failing to accept or obey proper authority. In the military, an enlisted man who insults an officer could be accused of an *insubordinate* act.

> *Frank, not eager to be branded insubordinate, did his best to carry out the colonel's strange orders.*

insurgence *(in-SUR-junce), noun*
Revolt or uprising. An *insurgence* is a revolt against the government or existing authority.

> *The insurgence against the dictator's regime was welcomed enthusiastically by the country's farmers.*

integral *(IN-tuh-grul), adjective*
Acting as a constituent and essential member of a whole. *Integral* also carries a number of technical and mathematical definitions not in common usage.

> *Jane played an integral role in the production's success.*

intercession *(in-ter-SESH-un), noun*
An instance of pleading in favor of another person or party. To *intercede* is to act or speak in someone's behalf; intercession is mediation in a conflict in behalf of another.

> *France's intercession is credited by many with brining the crisis to a peaceful conclusion.*

interim *(IN-ter-im), noun*
The meantime. An *interim* is the period of time between one event and another.

> *The interim--which lasted over a month--was filled with work and planning in preparation for the second series of meetings.*

intermittent *(in-tur-MIT-nt), adjective*
Characterized by a cycle of stopping and starting. An *intermittent* storm is one that comes and goes.

Frank was bothered by an intermittent pain in his ankle.

intransigent *(in-TRAN-si-junt), adjective*
Uncompromising; determined to remain beyond appeal or negotiation. Someone unyielding to any change is *intransigent.*

> *The intransigent union negotiator seemed fully prepared to see the talks collapse.*

intrepid *(in-TREP-id), adjective*
Brave. Those who are fearless and show great courage are *intrepid.*

> *The intrepid climber made her way down the icy mountain alone.*

intrinsic *(in-TRIN-zik), adjective*
In the essential nature of a thing. Something *intrinsic* is fundamental in character.

> *The intrinsic value of gold was one of the few common economic factors the nations could take advantage of.*

introspection *(in-tro-SPEK-shun), noun*
Self-examination; interior meditation. To think closely on one's feelings, thoughts, and inclinations is to spend time in *introspection.*

> *The weekend at the cabin provided Clive with an opportunity for some much-needed introspection.*

inundate *(IN-un-date), verb*
To flood. To *inundate* is to engulf as in a torrent or flood.

> *The operator knew she would be inundated with calls that day.*

invective *(in-VEK-tiv), noun*
Abusive language. *Invective* is denunciatory or overly harsh speech or writing.

> *Clark's stream of invective near the end of the meeting was totally uncalled for.*

inveigh *(in-VAY), verb*
To protest strongly. *Inveigh* is usually followed by *against*.

> *The crowd inveighed against the governor's decision to commute Davidson's sentence.*

inveterate *(in-VET-er-ut), adjective*
Deep-rooted. A persisting or long-established habit is an *inveterate* one.

> *Mike is an inveterate gambler; his marriage suffered greatly because of it.*

invocation *(in-vuh-KAY-shun), noun*
The process or act of *invoking*. An invocation is a call to a higher power (usually God) for help.

> *The priest offered a special invocation at the beginning of the service.*

irascible *(ih-RASS-uh-bul), adjective*
Easily angered. Those who are prone to fits of temper are *irascible*.

> *Sebastian, an irascible man, did his best to put on a show of conviviality when he visited his in-laws, most of whom irritated him.*

iridescent *(ear-ih-DESS-unt), adjective*
Possessing rainbowlike colors. *Iridescent* can also mean "altering in hue when viewed from different angles or moved."

> *The iridescent light of the prism flooded Newton's shuttered room.*

jejune *(ji-JOON), adjective*
Dull or lackluster. *Jejune* can also mean immature or lacking in insight.

> *Ralph's jejune fantasies of stardom brought only laughs of derision from his friends.*

jettison *(JET-ih-sun), verb*
To cast off or overboard. When a captain *jettisons* items from a

boat, he is sacrificing their value for the advantage of decreased weight on the ship. Similarly, to *jettison* can be to abandon something once thought valuable that has become a burden.

> *The project seemed promising initially, but now, with the looming possibility they could be accused of conflict of interest, Ted and Jan decided to jettison their plans.*

jingoistic *(jin-go-ISS-tik), adjective*
Aggressively and overbearingly patriotic. A jingo is a person whose patriotism is expressed in bellicose rhetoric (for instance, injunctions to prepare for war). Someone who is *jingoistic* is blindly and aggressively nationalistic.

> *Such jingoistic babbling can hardly be said to pass for decent advice to a head of state.*

jocular *(JOK-yoo-lur), adjective*
Joking; facetious. A *jocular* suggestion is one made in jest.

> *The jocular nature of the essay is not likely to win its author many adherents.*

jocund *(JOK-und), adjective*
Given to merriment. Someone who possesses a cheery disposition is *jocund*.

> *Tim's jocund personality made him the life of the party.*

jostle *(JOS-l), verb*
To bump or disrupt by means of incidental contact. To make one's way by elbowing or pushing (as through a crowd) is to *jostle*.

> *Mark jostled through the crowd, but could not find Sharon.*

judicature *(JOO-di-kuh-choor), noun*
The authority of jurisdiction of a court of law. The rank, function, or authority of a judge is referred to as the judge's *judicature*.

> *This case is in fact within my judicature, despite counsel's arguments to the contrary.*

jurisprudence *(joor-iss-PROO-dnce), noun*
The science of law. *Jurisprudence* is the philosophy behind legal practice.

> *Casey's study of jurisprudence lasted for three long years.*

juxtapose *(JUK-stuh-pose), verb*
To place side by side for comparison. To *juxtapose* is to align (usually two objects) for comparison or contrast.

> *He juxtaposed the two paragraphs at the end of each essay and found himself looking at the strongest evidence yet that plagiarism had occurred.*

keynote *(KEE-note), noun*
A prime theme, subject, or underlying element. A *keynote* address is given on a topic of relevance to a specific audience.

> *The keynote speaker addressed the many problems related to productivity that faced our organization.*

kibosh *(KYE-bosh), noun*
The act of halting or squelching. To put the *kibosh* on something is to stop it. Literally, a *kibosh* is a spell that brings about the doom of something.

> *We had wanted to go to the baseball game, but Ryan-- who's bored by the sport--put the kibosh on that pretty quickly.*

kinesiology *(kih-nee-see-OL-uh-jee), noun*
The study of physical movement and musculature. *Kinesiology* is the science concerned with the movement of muscles and related physical conditioning.

> *Only an expert in kinesiology could provide insight into Carl's illness.*

kinetic *(kih-NET-ik), adjective*
Pertaining to motion. *Kinetic* energy is the energy associated with the movement of a system or body.

> *The artist's kinetic sculptures captured spectator interest by means of grand sweeps, sudden plunges of pendulums, and dropping globes.*

kudos *(KOO-dos), noun*
Honor or accolades. The word *kudos*, occasionally used with a singular verb, is more commonly construed as a plural noun.

> *The kudos he received for his first novel were nothing compared to the glowing reviews that greeted his second.*

laconic *(luh-KON-ik), adjective*
Of few words. Speech that is concise or terse is *laconic*.

> *Cooper's performances are laconic, but all the more powerful for their terseness.*

laggard *(LAG-urd), noun*
One who lags behind or loiters. A *laggard* fails to keep up.

> *We have completed our part of the project, Mr. Miller; it is the laggards in the accounting department you should be reprimanding.*

lambaste *(LAM-baste), verb*
To reprimand sharply or attack verbally. *Lambaste* originally meant "to beat harshly."

> *What a lambasting he received from his mother for coming home late!*

lamentation *(lam-en-TAY-shun), noun*
An expression of mourning. Originally, a *lament* was a song or poem expressing grief; a lamentation is the act of expressing grief and sorrow.

> *Karl heard groans of lamentation from his mother's room.*

languid *(LANG-gwid), adjective*
Listless; lacking vitality. That which lacks force or vigor is *languid*.

> *Robert's languid demeanor was mistaken by some for a lack of intelligence.*

largess *(lar-ZHESS), noun*
Generously bestowed gifts. *Largess* (sometimes spelled *largesse*)

can also refer to a generous nature.

> *Her father's largess was the only thing standing between Barbara and bankruptcy.*

lascivious *(luh-SIV-ee-us), adjective*
Wanton or lustful. That which excites sexual desires is *lascivious*.

> *Grandmother Jones, upon being informed that the dancers at the club had done a can-can for us, denounced such lascivious goings on.*

latent *(LATE-nt), adjective*
Potential. A person with dormant abilities in sketching could be said to have *latent* artistic talent.

> *Paul's own latent musical ability was one of the main reasons he started the classical music club.*

laudatory *(LAW-duh-tore-ee), adjective*
Giving praise. A *laudatory* speech is one that praises or glorifies.

> *John's laudatory remarks really motivated the sales force.*

laureate *(LORE-ee-ut), adjective and noun*
Honored as a result of achievements. As a noun, *laureate* refers to a person who has been singled out for a particular high honor or award.

> *The group included a remarkable cross-section of accomplished scientists, some of whom were Nobel laureates.*

lethargic *(luh-THAR-jik), adjective*
Sluggish; inactive to such a degree as to resemble sleep or unconsciousness. A *lethargic* person is difficult to rouse to action.

> *After many long hours of work, Pat and Corey stared at each other, lethargic but unable to accept the necessity of calling it a night.*

levity *(LEH-vih-tee)*, *noun*
Lightness; insubstantiality. *Levity* often refers to inappropriately idle or humorous chatter.

> *Gentlemen, with all due respect, we face a crisis; this is no time for levity.*

lexicon *(LEK-sih-kon)*, *noun*
A dictionary composed for a specific, narrowly defined (professional) audience. *Lexicon* can also mean the vocabulary associated with a specific discipline or group.

> *Arthur, though not a doctor, was well versed in the lexicon of medicine.*

liaison *(lee-ay-ZON)*, *noun*
A communication channel. Also: A person who acts as a go-between or formal representative. Also: a romantic affair. *Liaison* is often used to describe the meetings of lovers, but it applies equally to formal organizational or bureaucratic contact.

> *Captain Morse was met by an Air Force liaison within minutes of his arrival.*

libation *(li-BAY-shun)*, *noun*
An alcoholic beverage offered or accepted in celebration. (The word is usually used facetiously, as if to exaggerate the supposed formality of an informal occasion.) Originally, a *libation* was a liquid offering at a formal religious rite.

> *Will you join us in a libation, Charles?*

lissome *(LISS-um)*, *adjective*
Supple. Something that is easily bent is *lissome*.

> *The lissome young gymnast's body seemed to defy the laws of physics.*

litany *(LIT-uh-nee)*, *noun*
Something (especially a list or a single sentence) related incessantly in an unwavering manner. A *litany* is a responsive prayer service within the Catholic church marked by much repetition.

> *We listened to Greta recite the usual litany of problems*

in the marketing department.

litigious *(lih-TIJ-us), adjective*
Overly inclined to engage in lawsuits. *Litigious* can also mean "of or pertaining to litigation."

> *Mr. Green, a litigious businessman in our town, once had seven cases pending at the same time.*

liturgy *(LIH-tur-jee), noun*
Worshipful ritual, especially the formal Christian service of the Eucharist. *Liturgy* is the accepted public form of religious worship.

> *Pat's attempts to reformulate the liturgy in her church were greeted with great skepticism by the more conservative worshipers.*

livid *(LIH-vid), adjective*
Extremely angry; infuriated. Literally, *livid* means discolored (as from a bruise). To say someone is *livid* in the sense of being angry is really to say his anger is so acute as to cause a change in his coloring.

> *Caroline was livid after she realized she had been swindled.*

locution *(loe-KYOO-shun), noun*
Style of speaking. A *locution* is also a particular word, expression, or phrase.

> *Martin's British locution would be a real asset during the many media appearances he would make over the next few years.*

logistics *(loe-JIS-tiks), noun*
The essential details of how something is to be accomplished. In military usage, *logistics* is the discipline addressing supply and procurement.

> *Jane knew the trip could not begin until the logistics were worked out.*

loquacious *(loe-KWAY-shuss), adjective*
Extremely talkative. Someone prone to nervous chatter could be

said to be *loquacious*.

> *Michael proved a loquacious houseguest; Mrs. Stevens did the best she could to manage his one-sided conversational torrents.*

Lothario *(lo-THAR-ee-oe), noun*
A seducer. The word *Lothario* originated from the name of a character in *The Fair Penitent*, a play (1703) by Nicholas Rowe.

> *Ryan is friendly, I'll admit, but he is certainly no Lothario.*

lucid *(LOO-sid), adjective*
Intelligible. *Lucid* can also refer to a clear mental state.

> *Although he lost consciousness for a few minutes, Glenn was lucid before the ambulance arrived.*

ludicrous *(LOO-dih-kruss), adjective*
Absurd to the point of being laughable. Something that is obviously implausible or impractical could be considered *ludicrous*.

> *Your proposal that I accept a 75% pay cut is ludicrous, Mr. Robinson.*

lugubrious *(loo-GOO-bree-us), adjective*
Mournful in the extreme. *Lugubrious* refers to something or someone mournful to an inappropriate degree.

> *You may consider Steven's poems "dark"; to me, they are simply lugubrious.*

lurid *(LOOR-id), adjective*
Gruesome or sensationalistic. Something likely to elicit horror, lust, shock, or disgust could be considered *lurid*.

> *The lurid illustrations made it clear to Pamela that this was no children's book she had bought.*

lustrous *(LUS-truss), adjective*
Radiant; shining. *Lustrous* refers to that which possesses a sheen or glow. Lustrous can also mean "brilliant" in the sense

of outstanding or exceptional.

Gina's lustrous eyes shimmered in the candlelight.

macabre *(muh-KAH-bruh), adjective*
Horrifying; reminiscent of death. A *macabre* story is one that focuses on morbid, grisly subjects.

The old man's macabre tales frightened the children.

machination *(mak-uh-NAY-shun), noun*
A conniving plot. A crafty scheme meant to achieve an illicit end is a *machination*.

Carrie was familiar with Desmond's machinations when it came to winning raises.

macrocosm *(MAK-ruh-koz-um), noun*
A representation on a large scale; the universe envisioned in its totality. In addition, a large system that reflects one of its component systems is a *macrocosm*.

Some early astronomers obviously believed the physical universe to be a a macrocosm of existing social and religious structures.

magnate *(MAG-nayt), noun*
An industrial leader. A *magnate* is a powerful business figure.

Your Honor, I am no communications magnate; I run a small town newspaper.

malady *(MAL-uh-dee), noun*
An illness or unwholesome condition. A *malady* is a disorder or disease causing discomfort.

Jason's malady, if it had gone undiagnosed, could have taken his life.

maleficence *(muh-LEF-ih-sence), noun*
The undertaking of evil or harmful acts. That which is mischevious or rooted in ill will could be said to

possess *maleficence*.

> *The long-ignored maleficence of the county's corrupt prison system was finally exposed by a rookie Globe reporter.*

malevolent *(muh-LEV-uh-lent)*, *adjective*
Malicious. Someone who is unrepentantly and viciously ill-willed is *malevolent*.

> *Glen cast a malevolent glance at his opponent.*

malice *(MAL-iss)*, *noun*
The desire to commit harmful or unfair acts. Someone who intends to commit an act known to be immoral, unlawful, or likely to cause harm shows *malice*.

> *The defendant clearly showed malice in stating that he intended to kill Mrs. Powers.*

malignant *(muh-LIG-nunt)*, *adjective*
Posing a serious threat or harm. A *malignant* tumor can cause death.

> *They had feared the growth would be found malignant, but it turned out to be benign.*

malinger *(muh-LING-ger)*, *verb*
To avoid work by making up excuses. Someone who pretends to be ill or injured in order to avoid effort or duty can be said to *malinger*.

> *"There will be no malingering in this office," the new supervisor said sternly.*

malleable *(MAL-ee-uh-bull)*, *adjective*
Easily shaped or reformed. That which can be easily altered or influenced is *malleable*.

> *It is best to go over the company's rather odd sick leave policy on the employee's first day; people are more malleable in such a setting.*

mandate *(MAN-date), noun*
Authoritative command, endorsement, or instruction. A *mandate* is also an order issued by one court of law to another, lower court.

> *Having received only 40% of the vote nationwide, President Lincoln could hardly claim a national mandate for his policies.*

maniacal *(muh-NYE-uh-kull), adjective*
Insane. Also: overly emphatic or nervous. *Maniacal* is often used ironically to describe a person's near-fanatical devotion to a certain pursuit.

> *Chuck's obsession with baseball statistics bordered on the maniacal.*

maraud *(muh-ROD), verb*
To wander in search of booty. To loot or invade for treasure is to *maraud.*

> *The ship was waylaid by marauding pirates on the fourteenth of May.*

martial *(MAR-shull), adjective*
Appropriate to wartime. *Martial* law is the imposition of military control over a civilian population. (We describe disciplines such as judo and karate--which focus on hand-to-hand combat--as *martial* arts.)

> *After capturing Richmond, the commander issued an order placing it under martial law.*

martyrdom *(MAR-ter-dum), noun*
The condition of having suffered death as a martyr. A person who has attained *martyrdom* has died or been killed for a principle or cause, and has come to be regarded with reverence by others as a result.

> *Many say that John Brown's martyrdom served his cause more effectively than anything he did at Harper's Ferry.*

masticate *(MASS-tih-kate), verb*
To chew. To *masticate* is to knead and grind with the teeth.

> *Grandpa, always an extravagant speaker, referred to his dentures as his "masticating companions."*

matriarch *(MAY-tree-ark), noun*
A woman who presides over a family or group. A woman who holds the dominant position in an organization or family can be said to be the group's *matriarch*.

> *Millicent Bryant, matriarch of the large Bryant family, made her customary speech at the reunion.*

maverick *(MAV-er-ik), noun*
Free and independent of outside association or contact. A *maverick* is an independent-minded person who resists the influence of a group. (The word referred originally to a horse or steer that escapes from a herd and runs alone.)

> *Although Ryan portrayed himself as a maverick politician, he owed favors to the same special interest groups his opponent did.*

mawkish *(MAW-kish), adjective*
Overly sentimental. Something that is emotional or maudlin is *mawkish*.

> *Daytime soap operas irritated Melanie; she found them mawkish and unbelievable.*

meander *(mee-AN-der), verb*
To follow a turning and winding path. To *meander* is to wander idly without a set goal.

> *Jack, lost without his shopping list, meandered helplessly through the aisles of the supermarket.*

megalomania *(meg-uh-lo-MAY-nee-uh), noun*
Delusions of wealth and/or power. Literally, *megalomania* is a psychopathological condition in which a person is obsessed with fantasies of riches or authority. The word is also used to

describe people whose ambitions and sense of self-importance are overblown.

> *Some have interpreted the tycoon's purchase of the old castle as an uncharacteristically bad real estate deal; I see it as pure megalomania.*

melancholy *(MEL-un-kol-lee) noun*
Sadness or depression. *Melancholy* can also refer to a subdued, reflective, or contemplative spirit.

> *A melancholy-looking girl walked by the seashore, apparently lost in her thoughts.*

mellifluous *(muh-LIF-loo-us), adjective*
Flowing sweetly and smoothly. *Mellifluous* describes a smooth, sweet sensation.

> *Jane's mellifluous cello playing was the envy of the other musicians.*

melodious *(muh-LOW-dee-us), adjective*
Pleasant or agreeable to the ear. *Melodious* refers to that which features a pleasing succession of sounds.

> *The melodious tones of his mother's voice always reminded Wayne of his childhood.*

mendacious *(men-DAY-shuss), adjective*
Lying or false. Someone who tells falsehoods could be said to be *mendacious*.

> *Clark's mendacious habits will catch up with him; one of these days his lies will be exposed.*

mentor *(MEN-tor), noun*
A counselor or teacher. In contemporary use, *mentor* usually refers to a senior figure (in business or politics, for instance) who aids the progress of a junior figure's career.

> *Bart respected and revered his mentor, but he knew the time had come to move on to another company.*

mesmerize *(MEZ-mur-ize), verb*
To hypnotize. *Mesmerize* is derived from the name of a 19th-century physician, Franz Mesmer, whose early work in the field we know call hypnotism won him acclaim in Austria and throughout Europe.

> *It is said that Huey Long mesmerized his audiences more with his style of speaking than with the substance of his speeches.*

metamorphosis *(met-uh-MORE-fuh-siss), noun*
A transformation, as by magic or other supernatural influence. Someone or something undergoing a change in form can be said to undergo a *metamorphosis*.

> *Darryl's friends viewed his entry into reactionary politics with some concern; because of his past history, they feared his metamorphosis into a militant.*

microcosm *(MY-kro-koz-um), noun*
A model that reflects a larger thing. A *microcosm* is a small system roughly comparable to a larger system.

> *A microcosm of society is represented on board the Pequod in Melville's novel Moby Dick.*

millenium *(muh-LEN-ee-um), noun*
A period of one thousand years. In Christian theology, the *Millenium* is a thousand-year span during which Christ is to rule human affairs.

> *The members of the small church prayed for the early arrival of the Millenium.*

misanthropy *(miss-ANN-thruh-pee), noun*
Hatred of mankind. *Misanthropy* refers to contempt for the human race.

> *Scrooge's misanthropy was to end that Christmas Eve.*

miscegenation *(mih-sej-uh-NAY-shun), noun*
Interbreeding between members of different racial groups.

Miscegenation was once a crime in parts of the United States.

> *The musical* Show Boat *was daring for its time; certainly no previous show on Broadway had dared to examine an issue as sensitive as miscegenation.*

misconstrue *(miss-kun-STROO), verb*
To misinterpret. To analyze and in so doing make an error is to *misconstrue*.

> *I am afraid my intentions with regard to your daughter have been misconstrued.*

misogamy *(mih-SOG-uh-mee) noun*
Hatred of marriage. Someone who holds only contempt for the institution of marriage and refuses to take a husband or wife could be said to practice *misogamy*.

> *After his divorce, Brent's mistrust of marriage bordered on misogamy.*

misogyny *(my-SOJ-uh-nee), noun*
Hatred of women. Someone who holds a bitter contempt for all women practices *misogyny*.

> *Rousseau's prejudices against women frequently cross the line and harden into outright misogyny.*

mitigate *(MIH-tih-gate), verb*
To moderate. To *mitigate* is to lessen in impact or degree, or to cause to become less intense or severe.

> *The international situation had seemed tense until a number of mitigating factors--notably the overthrow of General Sanchez--came into play.*

mnemonic *(ni-MON-ik), adjective and noun*
Meant to aid in memory. As a noun, a *mnemonic* is a device (a rhyme, for instance) meant to make memorizing easier.

> *The flashcards serve only as mnemonic devices; they*

cannot, by themselves, instill any understanding of mathematical processes.

modulate *(MOJ-uh-late)*, verb
To vary. In music, to *modulate* is to change from one key to another.

> *The radio announcer began modulating his voice in order to counter criticisms that he spoke in a monotone.*

mollify *(MOL-uh-fy)*, verb
To allay (a person's) anger. *Mollify* can also mean "to lessen the impact of."

> *The umpire's attempts to mollify the two screaming managers with some risque humor were to no avail.*

monochromatic *(mon-owe-kru-MAT-ik)*, adjective
Of a single color. Something that features varying shades of only one hue in addition to the background hue (usually white) is *monochromatic.*

> *The sweep and power of Adams's monochromatic photography proves how much can be accomplished with a roll of black-and-white film.*

monogamy *(muh-NOG-uh-mee)*, noun
The practice of being faithful to a single married partner. The opposite of *monogamy* is *polygamy.*

> *The priest reminded the couple that they should not get married without thoroughly examining their feelings toward maintaining a life of monogamy.*

monograph *(MON-uh-graff)*, noun
A scholarly article or essay on a certain topic. A *monograph* is usually intended for an academic audience and not for the general public.

> *Peterson's monograph on theoretical physics was well received in the scientific community, although it certainly makes for tough reading for the layman.*

monolithic *(mon-uh-LITH-ik) adjective*
Unwieldy or cumbersome; huge. A monolith is a massive block of stone or other marker (such as a sculpture) that shows solidity and uniformity; something that is monolithic calls to mind the imposing nature of a *monolith*.

> *The monolithic presence of IBM in the computer field is sobering enough to make any competitor think twice before introducing a new product.*

monorail *(MON-oh-rail), noun*
A train that moves on a single rail. Short-run *monorails* have been constructed in Houston, Seattle, and the Disneyland and Disney World theme parks.

> *We'll drive to the station and then take the monorail into the downtown district.*

moribund *(MORE-uh-bund), adjective*
About to die. *Moribund* means, literally, "bound toward death."

> *The Confederacy lay in ruins, its currency worthless, its capital desecrated, its once proud fighting force moribund.*

morose *(muh-ROCE), adjective*
Frightening or gloomy. *Morose* refers to that which is melancholy or sullen in spirit.

> *Carl knew his company was headed for bankruptcy; he spent several long morose nights alone staring silently at the accounting ledger.*

mortify *(MORE-tih-fy), verb*
To humiliate. To *mortify* is also to discipline (one's body) through austerity or self-denial.

> *Mrs. Jones's mother was mortified at the thought of her daughter attending the dance unescorted.*

motley *(MOT-lee), adjective*
Of diverse composition. Something that shows many colors or

facets could be said to be *motley*. (The word has come to carry negative overtones of raggedness or lack of union.)

> *It was Frederick's job to mold the motley assemblage he had been given into a powerful fighting force.*

multifaceted *(mul-tee-FASS-ih-tid), adjective*
Possessing many facets or dimensions. Someone who has many talents is *multifaceted*.

> *Joan, a multifaceted writer, had published poems, essays, and novels.*

multifarious *(mul-tih-FARE-ee-uss), adjective*
Made of many components. Something that has a large number of parts is *multifarious*.

> *From the air, New York's multifarious skyline sparkled--as if beckoning to Mary to try her hand there.*

mundane *(mun-DANE), adjective*
Ordinary or everyday. That which is common or pertains to the concerns of the workaday world is *mundane*.

> *Everett's concerns were mundane enough: keep a roof over his head, track down the occasional meal.*

munificent *(myoo-NIF-ih-sent), adjective*
Generous. Someone who has liberal habits of giving could be said to be *munificent*.

> *The munificent old widow gave abundantly to charity.*

muse *(MYOOZ), verb*
To meditate (about a topic). To *muse* over something is to consider it closely.

> *Phyllis mused over the advertising campaign for some days before finally approving it.*

myopia *(mye-OH-pee-uh), noun*
Inability to see close things clearly. Figuratively, to suffer from

myopia is to lack foresight.

> *My feeling is that by turning down that project, Fenster showed once again that he suffers from myopia when it comes to marketing new consumer products.*

myriad *(MEER-ee-ud), adjective*

Innumerable. To say there are *myriad* reasons to do something is to say there are too many to list.

> *Edward's responsibilities were myriad, but his authority was almost nonexistent.*

nabob *(NAY-bob), noun*

A wealthy person who is accustomed to luxury. Originally, a *nabob* was a person who returned to Europe from India with great riches.

> *All the city's nabobs, potentates, and intellectual stars showed up for Iris's party.*

nanosecond *(NAN-oh-sek-und), noun*

One billionth of a second. *Nanosecond* is also used loosely to describe the shortest conceivable period of time.

> *I promise, Casey, I'll get that package to you the nanosecond it comes in.*

napalm *(NAY-pom), noun*

A type of burning plastic used as a weapon in military conflicts. *Napalm* is disfiguring and excruciatingly painful.

> *The United States used napalm extensively during the Vietnam war.*

narcissistic *(nar-sis-SIS-tik), adjective*

Possessed by self-love. Someone whose egotism replaces (or seems to replace) attention to others can be said to be *narcissistic*.

> *Self-promotion is one thing; the narcissistic zeal with which Gerald asserts himself is quite another.*

narcolepsy *(NAR-ko-lep-see), noun*
The disorder of suddenly and unpredictably falling asleep.
Someone who has *narcolepsy* is prone to unexpectedly
succumb to the urge to sleep.

> *After learning he suffered from narcolepsy, Brian realized
> how dangerous it would be for him to drive, and
> voluntarily returned his license to the Registry.*

narcoma *(nar-KO-muh), noun*
A hazy state between sleep and wakefulness reminiscent of or
signalling use of narcotics. To be in a *narcoma* is to be in a
partially concious state associated with drug use.

> *Because she had worked in a city emergency room for
> four years, Ellen knew that the boy had slipped into
> narcoma.*

nascent *(NAY-sunt), adjective*
Emerging. *Nascent* refers to something's early stages of coming
into existence.

> *The nascent republic had few if any established
> democratic traditions.*

nebulous *(NEB-yoo-luss), adjective*
Vague. If something is cloudy or hazy it is *nebulous*. The word
is derived from nebula (a wispy mass of interstellar gas or
dust).

> *The party's nebulous doctrines were difficult for Judith to
> comprehend.*

necrology *(nek-ROL-uh-jee), noun*
A list of people who have recently died. A *necrology* can also
be an obituary.

> *Benjamin scoured the long necrology for the name of his
> father, but it was not there.*

necromancy *(NEK-ruh-man-see), noun*
The supposed practice of gaining insight by means of

communication with the dead. *Necromancy* can also mean "witchcraft."

> *Necromancy is still a part of many tribal rituals on the island.*

nefarious *(nuh-FARE-ee-us), adjective*
Evil. That which is manifestly wicked or unjust is *nefarious*.

> *To what nefarious end has this information been withheld?*

nemesis *(NEM-i-sis), noun*
An opponent motivated by revenge. A person's *nemesis* is one who will stop at nothing to "settle a score."

> *Things looked bleak: Harold's nemesis, Mike, was in charge of all hiring decisions.*

neolithic *(nee-oh-LITH-ik), adjective*
Of or pertaining to the latter part of the Stone Age, when ground stone weapons and tools first came into use. To dismiss something as *neolithic* is to say it is so unsophisticated as to belong to a much earlier era.

> *In these days of computers and word processors, many consider the old-fashioned manual typewriter positively neolithic.*

neophyte *(NEE-uh-fite), noun*
A recent convert. *Neophyte* often refers to someone whose newfound zeal is not balanced by experience.

> *Jane, a relative neophyte, found little warmth in her discussions with the other, more knowledgeable members of the group.*

ne plus ultra *(nay plooce OOL-truh), noun*
The highest possible embodiment (of something). *Ne plus ultra* is Latin for "Do not go beyond this point."

> *Many consider* Oedipus Rex *the drama's* ne plus ultra.

nepotism *(NEP-uh-tiz-um), noun*
Favoritism toward relatives in professional matters. *Nepotism* is generally considered unethical.

> *When it was learned that he had three nephews on his staff, Jerry was instantly accused of nepotism by his boss.*

nether *(NETH-ur), adjective*
Lower; removed. The *nether* regions of something are the parts that lie beneath or beyond the main part.

> *Dante takes the reader on a journey to the nether regions of hell.*

neurology *(noo-ROL-uh-gee), noun*
The study of the nervous system and its diseases. A *neurologist* is a doctor whose specialty is neurology.

> The Man Who Mistook His Wife For A Hat *is a fascinating account of neurological disorders written for the layman.*

nexus *(NEK-sus), noun*
A linkage or connection. A *nexus* can also be the means by which two or more things are connected

> *The stars in the cluster formed a nexus one could trace across the sky.*

niggardly *(NIG-urd-lee), adjective*
Stingy. *Niggardly* refers to an unwillingness to give, share, or spend.

> *The niggardly merchant turned the begging man away with an impatient wave of the hand.*

nirvana *(nir-VAW-nuh), noun*
A point or state of spiritual perfection. *Nirvana* has a number of theological definitions, but is usually understood to mean "a transcendent state beyond the concerns of existence."

Some of the monks had meditated and maintained complete silence for years in an attempt to achieve nirvana.

noblesse oblige *(no-BLESS oh-BLEEZH), noun*

Benevolence befitting a person's dignity and/or possession of high birth. *Noblesse oblige* is from the French for "nobility obliges." The phrase usually refers to charitable actions or disposition toward those in classes perceived as low.

A sense of noblesse oblige, not desire for headlines, motivates the Beal family's admirable tradition of giving and volunteerism.

nocturnal *(nok-TUR-nal), adjective*

Pertaining to night. Activities that occur only at night are *nocturnal.*

Owls are perhaps the best known species of nocturnal birds.

nom de guerre *(nom duh GARE), noun*

A name taken or bestowed during wartime. *Nom de guerre* is French for "wartime name."

Fred's nom de guerre in the regiment was Rookie, and he did not like it.

nomenclature *(NO-men-klat-cher), noun*

A system of names for purposes of organization. A *nomenclature* is a technical, professional, or artistic set or system of names in a given discipline.

Harold had a good grasp of the fundamental principles of chemistry, but his knowledge of the nomenclature of chemical compounds was weak.

nonchalance *(NON-shu-lonce), noun*

The quality of being unconcerned with worldly cares. A cool, carefree person can be said to be *nonchalant.*

Astaire's nonchalance was appealing to the audience of

the time, which was on the whole weighed down with the many cares of the Depression.

nonentity *(non-EN-ti-tee), noun*
Something that does not exist. A *nonentity* is a vacuum or a purely imaginary thing. Nonentity is sometimes used insultingly to describe a person of little importance.

You may safely regard this clause of the contract as a nonentity; it is obsolete and completely unenforceable.

nonfeasance *(non-FEEZ-unce), noun*
Failure to perform (a given duty). Someone who is bound to act in a certain way and does not is guilty of *nonfeasance.*

The failure of the passersby to aid the injured woman was a heartrending example of urban apathy and nonfeasance.

nonpareil *(non-puh-RELL), noun*
A person without parallel or equal. *Nonpareil* can also mean "a flat chocolate covered with colored sugar."

Frank is hardly the nonpareil as a mystery writer he makes himself out to be.

non sequitur *(non-SEK-wi-tur), noun and adjective*
Something that does not follow logically. A statement that has no basis in what has gone before is considered a *non sequitur.*

The professor pointed out the many non sequiturs contained in the pamphlet.

noxious *(NOK-shuss), adjective*
Harmful; injurious. That which has a corrupting or debilitating influence is *noxious.*

The noxious weed soon took over the entire crop, which eventually failed.

nouveau riche *(noo-voh-REESH), noun and adjective*
Someone recently wealthy. *Nouveau riche* is often used to

describe those whose newfound wealth brings with it a tactless or overbearing attitude.

> *The escapades of the nouveau riche are not the concern of this column.*

nubile *(NOO-bile), adjective*
Sexually mature and/or prepared for marriage. *Nubile* is used almost exclusively in reference to young women; there is no exact parallel to describe young men.

> *Art looked at his "baby" daughter Marie and realized that she had somehow become a nubile young woman of eighteen.*

nugatory *(NOO-guh-toe-ree), adjective*
Worthless or in vain. That which is trifling or pointless is *nugatory*.

> *I'm afraid the edict of the High Commissioner has rendered your request to have the prisoner freed nugatory.*

numerology *(noo-muh-ROL-uh-jee), noun*
The supposed practice of divining the future through analyzing the occult significance of numbers. *Numerology* is not the same as the science of mathematics.

> *Judy's interest in numerology is the latest in a series of mystic doings; she was very big on Tarot cards last week.*

numismatics *(noo-miz-MAT-iks), noun*
Coin or currency collecting. *Numismatics* can also include the collecting of paper money or medals.

> *I suppose my decision to put aside my newly minted Susan B. Anthony dollar coin marked my first foray into numismatics.*

obfuscate (OB-fuss-kate), verb

To muddy or confuse an issue. Someone who *obfuscates* makes every effort to muddle facts important to someone else's judgment or decision.

> *The defense has put up with enough of these attempts to obfuscate, Your Honor.*

obligatory (uh-BLIG-uh-tore-ee), adjective

Required as an obligation. To say a duty is *obligatory* is to say that one is bound by morality, law, or tradition to perform it.

> *The coaches, who hated each other bitterly, nevertheless exchanged the obligatory handshakes at the end of the game.*

oblique (oh-BLEEK), adjective

Angled; indirect. To make an *oblique* reference to something is to mention it glancingly, leaving the listener unclear as to the nature or context of the thing referred to.

> *The witness's description was too oblique to be of any use to the police.*

oblivion (uh-BLIV-ee-un), noun

The state of being beyond memory and utterly forgotten. To say something is in *oblivion* is to say it is lost to human recollection.

> *To Tim, the fact that his book was being allowed to go out of print meant that he as an author had been consigned to oblivion.*

oblivous (uh-BLIV-ee-uss), adjective

Not mindful. Someone who is *oblivious* displays little awareness of surroundings.

> *We warned Jan about the consequences of her actions, but she was oblivious to us.*

obsequious (ub-SEE-kwee-uss), adjective

Compliant and servile to superiors. Someone who takes a fawning, submissive demeanor in order to curry favor with those in authority could be said to be *obsequious*.

You may consider the waiter's attentions well meant; I find him obsequious.

obsolescence *(ob-suh-LESS-unce), noun*
The state or condition of becoming outdated. Planned *obsolescence* is the deliberate "underdesigning" of products or systems; the items are meant to wear out sooner than they might in order to make way for new items to fulfill essentially the same function.

The farm machinery's obsolescence was now hard for even Grandpa to deny.

obstinate *(OB-sti-nut), adjective*
Unyielding. Someone who holds firmly to an opinion, attitude, or approach despite obstacles could be said to be *obstinate*.

Melvin, obstinate to the end, refused to talk to Mr. Smith about settling the case out of court.

obtuse *(ob-TOOS), adjective*
Not sharp. *Obtuse* is most often used to describe a person whose powers of intellect or observation are poor.

Perhaps I'm being obtuse, but I'd like you to explain that last point again for me.

obviate *(OB-vee-ate), verb*
To make unnecessary. To *obviate* something is to avoid it by acting in anticipation.

The research department provided sufficient data; the problem was obviated before it reached crisis proportions.

occlude *(ob-KLOOD), verb*
To obstruct. Something that is closed or blocked off is *occluded*.

Mr. Ryan, who had a history of heart problems, died that night of a coronary occlusion.

octogenarean *(ok-tuh-juh-NARE-ee-un), noun*
A person in his or her eighties. An *octogenarean* is one who is between eighty and eighty-nine years old.

> *Mrs. Reardon, an octogenarean, attributes her longevity to drinking a glass of fruit juice every mornig.*

odyssey (ODD-uh-see), noun
A long journey that entails danger or adventure. *Odyssey* derives from Homer's poem The Odyssey, which describes such a journey undertaken by the character Odysseus.

> *The film* Easy Rider *recounts the oddysey of two counterculture motorcyclists in search of America.*

odious *(OH-dee-us), adjective*
Abhorrent. Something that stirs disgust or hatred could be said to be *odious*.

> *Such odious sentiments of racial prejudice have no place in this company.*

officious *(uh-FISH-uss), adjective*
Prone to offering one's services and/or insight, even when they are not requested or appropriate. Someone who is *officious* is meddlesome and overbearing.

> *Tom was certainly a generous host, but his officious nature was hard for me to live with after a week or two.*

ominous *(OM-ih-nuss), adjective*
Foreboding or menacing. Something that is *ominous* foretells the possibility of future harm or evil.

> *The day began with sunny weather, but by two p.m. an ominous sky threatened to ruin our outing.*

omniscient *(om-NISS-see-unt), adjective*
All-knowing. *Omniscient* refers to having absolute knowledge.

> *Contrary to what you may have heard, Professor Powers*

is not omnisicent; he still has a thing or two to learn about chairing the biology department.

omnivorous *(om-NIV-er-uss), adjective*
Accustomed to eating both animal and vegetable food items. *Omnivorous* (derived from the Latin for "eating everything") can also mean "voracious," in the sense of taking all that is offered.

The Cantonese, I am told, are omnivorous, and it is said that the traveler is best advised not to inquire too closely into exactly what he is eating.

onerous *(OWE-nur-uss), adjective*
Troublesome and burdensome. Something that entails heavy a obligation might be considered *onerous*.

This contract--a thoroughly one-sided agreement--is perhaps the most onerous document I have ever seen.

onomatopoeia *(on-uh-mot-uh-PEE-uh), noun*
The development of a word whose pronunciation imitates its main reference. The words "splat" and "buzz," for instance, are examples of *onomatopoeia*.

Over the centuries, the process of onomatopoeia has become an accepted part of the English language.

onus *(OWN-us), noun*
The burden of performing a task or duty. To say that the *onus* is on a person to do something is to say that he is responsible for doing it.

The onus of completing this long-delayed project now falls to you.

opaque *(oh-PAKE), adjective*
Impenetrable to light. That which does not allow light to pass through is *opaque*.

Karl was unable to make out exactly what was happening behind the opaque screen that had been set in front of him.

opine *(oh-PINE), verb*
To make one's opinion known. To *opine* is to state one's view.

> *Grant opined that he could take Vicksburg if the President would show patience in the undertaking.*

opprobrium *(uh-PRO-bree-um), noun*
Infamy. *Opprobrium* is disgrace resulting from shameful action.

> *Quentin knew that dropping out of school would bring only opprobrium from his father.*

optimal *(OP-tih-mul), adjective*
Best; favored. The *optimal* time for something is the best possible time.

> *As you know, we were not working in optimal conditions: it was snowing heavily and the wind was blowing at over 40 m.p.h.*

opulent *(OP-yoo-lent), adjective*
Rich. Something characterized by wealth or affluence (an extravagant dinner party, for instance) could be considered *opulent*.

> *Without the money from Powers, Hans knew he would be unable to maintain his opulent lifestyle.*

opus *(OPE-us), noun*
A major work (of art or literature). Opera is derived from one of the plural forms of *opus*. (In English, *opuses* is the accepted plural.)

> *Although he had been working on it for over a year and a half, the composer was less than halfway done with his opus.*

oracle *(OR-uh-kul), noun*
A means by which prophetic wisdom is imparted. *Oracle* is sometimes used figuratively to describe someone who is seen as offering completely dependable counsel or advice.

After Appomatox, Grant's words seemed (much to his surprise) to be regarded as having issued from an oracle.

ornate *(or-NATE), adjective*
Overwrought or decorated elaborately. That which is flashy or extravagantly ornamented is *ornate*.

The furniture in the living room was as ornate as it was uncomfortable.

oscillate *(OSS-uh-late), verb*
To waver between two (or more) points. Someone who alternates between available options and cannot come to a conclusion could be said to *oscillate*.

Hamlet oscillates between bravado and paralysis for much of the play.

osmosis *(oss-MOE-siss), noun*
The process of attaining something (knowledge, for instance) by gradual exposure to it, seemingly without conscious effort. In chemistry, *osmosis* describes the process by which fluids are dispersed and equalized in concentration through membranes.

Patricia boasted that she learned French not by taking a course, but through osmosis during a year she spent in Paris.

ossify *(OSS-ih-fye), verb*
To harden or become bonelike. Literally, *ossify* means "to change into a bone," but it is often used to describe a rigidity of outlook or opinion.

The creative team's concepts, which had originally seemed very promising, had ossified into a conventional set of ideas that no one found exciting.

ostensibly *(uh-STEN-sib-lee), adverb*
Seemingly; as represented. A reason *ostensibly* given for taking an action is the reason that, to all intents and purposes, one would associate with motivating the act.

He was ostensibly visiting the city on business; no one

ostentatious *(oss-ten-TAY-shuss), adjective*
Showy. Someone who makes a boastful display, or makes constant attempts to show off talents or possessions, could be said to be *ostentatious*.

> *You shouldn't take the Rolls to the party; it will be seen as ostentatious.*

ostracize *(OSS-truh-size), verb*
To exclude or banish. To *ostracize* someone is to exclude him from a social circle.

> *Desmond was ostracized from the group after the negative publicity his mother received.*

pacify *(PASS-ih-fie), verb*
To bring to a point of peace; to dissuade from anger or hostility. Someone who eases tensions or resolves conflicts *pacifies* a situation.

> *Her suggestion that she offer a written apology to the offended client seemed to pacify Mr. Peters.*

pagination *(paj-ih-NAY-shun), noun*
The numbers by which one marks the pages in a book. *Pagination* also refers to the sequence and arrangement of pages in a book.

> *The word processor paginated Jim's document flawlessly the first time.*

palatable *(PAL-uh-tuh-bull), adjective*
Agreeable in taste. *Palatable* can also mean "acceptable."

> *You have two options, Mr. Mayor, neither very palatable.*

palaver *(puh-LAV-er), noun*
A parley or conference. *Palaver* can also refer to charming but insubstantial talk meant to persuade or cajole.

Don't be taken in by Frank's palaver; he is not the agent for you.

palpable *(PALP-uh-bull), adjective*
Touchable or able to be perceived. That which is *palpable* is tangible or undeniably present.

A palpable sense of excitement filled the air of the city before the big game.

pandemic *(pan-DEM-ik), adjective*
Widespread. Something that is general, common, or all-encompassing could be said to be *pandemic*.

We must begin to appeal not to universal fears, but to pandemic human values.

pandemonium *(pan-duh-MOAN-ee-um), noun*
Chaos. *Pandemonium* refers to wild, uproarious, and noisy tumult.

Pandemonium broke out in the streets of the city after the local team won the pennant.

pander *(PAN-der), verb and noun*
To appeal to the worst in someone. Literally, a *pander* is a pimp.

Despite accusations that he was pandering to the voters, the candidate insisted on repeatedly raising the issue of his opponent's extramarital affairs.

pantheism *(PAN-thee-iz-um), noun*
A doctrine that espouses God's manifestation in all things. *Pantheism* tends to identify Deity with the natural world. The word derives from the Greek roots for "all" and "God."

It is fair to say that although she had no formal religious upbringing, Edith tended toward the pantheism she associated with certain Native American religious rites.

papal *(PAY-pull)*, *adjective*

Of or pertaining to the pope. A *papal* decree is one issued by the pope.

> *The actor was unable to obtain a papal audience, although he did meet with an archbishop while visiting the Vatican.*

paradigm *(PARE-uh-dime)*, *noun*

An example. A *paradigm* is an ideal instance or a pattern worthy of study.

> *There have been a number of presidencies well suited to times of national crisis, but Lincoln's is the paradigm.*

paradox *(PAIR-uh-doks)*, *noun*

A seemingly self-contradictory statement that expresses a valid idea or potentially true statement. *Paradox* can also mean "a conclusion that, while reached by conventional logical methods, nevertheless cancels itself out."

> *Before announcing the test grades, Mrs. Miller reminded her students of the paradox that a teacher often must be cruel in order to be kind.*

paragon *(PARE-uh-gone)*, *noun*

A peerless model or pattern of perfection. A *paragon*, unlike a *paradigm* (above) is an absolute--and often a hypothetical--standard.

> *Even if we could live our lives in accordance with the paragons of right living, would we not still experience conflict and misunderstanding with others?*

paralysis *(puh-RAL-ih-siss)*, *noun*

Loss or damage of movement ability; the loss of feeling in a part of the body due to disease or injury. *Paralysis* is used figuratively to refer to the inability of a person or institution to take action in a given situation.

> *Lacking firm direction from its founder, the company soon reached a state of paralysis.*

parameter (puh-RAM-uh-ter), noun
Limit or boundary. *Parameter* also has a technical meaning within the field of statistics, but this is not in common use.

>*Within these broad parameters, you are free to act as you see fit.*

parenthetical *(par-un-THET-ih-kul) adjective*
Contained within parentheses. Figuratively, something that qualifies or explains in a manner setting it off from a main idea is *parenthetical*.

>*I should add, as a parenthetical note, that I am donating all monies raised from these efforts to charity.*

parlance *(PAR-lunce), noun*
A way of speaking. Something that is in common *parlance* is familiar to most speakers.

>*The special parlance of the construction workers was difficult for Mort to decipher.*

paroxysm *(PARE-uk-siz-um), noun*
An outburst. A *paroxysm* is a sudden action or an incidence reminiscent of something explosive.

>*Joan broke out in paroxysms of laughter at Pete's joke.*

parsimonious *(par-suh-MOAN-ee-uss), adjective*
Stingy. Someone who is exceptionally frugal or thrifty could be considered *parsimonious*.

>*The old man's parsimonious ways were legend: it is said that in a lifetime of restaurant dining, he never once picked up a check.*

pastoral *(PAS-tur-ul), adjective*
Pertaining to life in the country. Pastoral also has religious connotations: a *pastoral* message is one to the clergy or people in a region from a bishop.

>*To many critics, the novel's pastoral setting jarred*

against its themes of urban angst.

pathos *(PAY-thos), noun*
A quality arousing or evoking pity or sorrow. To employ *pathos* is to act in a way meant to elicit tender sympathy from an observer.

> *Chaplin's development of pathos as a component of film comedy was one of his most significant achievements.*

patrimony *(PAT-rih-mo-nee), noun*
Heritage or legacy. Someone's *patrimony* can be either a financial inheritance or an ancestral heritage. (A *patrimony* can also be a church endowment.)

> *The will outlined patrimony payments totaling over one million dollars.*

paucity *(PAW-si-tee), noun*
Smallness of number. A *paucity* of something is a shortage or lack of it.

> *We were forced to head back down the mountain due to a paucity of supplies.*

peccadillo *(pek-uh-DILL-oh), noun*
A minor fault. *Pecadillo* comes from the Italian for "little sin."

> *Jane knew her peccadillo would be overlooked, but she could not put it out of her mind.*

pecuniary *(pi-KYOO-nee-air-ee), adjective*
Of or pertaining to money. That which consists of or concerns money is *pecuniary.*

> *Uncle Walter decided to stay with us for a few months owing, as he put it, to "pecuniary difficulties."*

pedagogue *(PED-uh-gog), noun*
An educator or schoolteacher. A *pedagogue* is a person who instructs.

Mr. Harper, a stern pedagogue, would not tolerate idle chatter in his class.

pedantic *(puh-DAN-tik), adjective*
Intellectually showy or overblown. A pedant is a person who makes a great display of knowledge; to be *pedantic* is to act in this way. *Pedantic* can also mean "overly concerned with formal rules."

I found James's pedantic manner quite condescending.

pejorative *(puh-JORE-uh-tiv), adjective*
Disparaging. That which downgrades or defames (usually a term or description) is *pejorative*.

When I said Lynn was a typical Massachusetts driver, I didn't mean that as a pejorative remark.

penultimate *(pen-UL-ti-mut), adjective*
Next-to-last. *Penultimate* is often thought to mean "final," but it does not.

The book's penultimate chapter gave no hint of the surprise ending the novel had in store.

penurious *(peh-NOOR-ee-uss), adjective*
Miserly. *Penurious* can also mean "lacking in means or extremely poor."

Joan, raised in comfortable surroundings, was not cut out for such a penurious lifestyle.

perambulate *(puh-RAM-byuh-late), verb*
To walk around. To *perambulate* is to stroll or saunter.

The elderly couple perambulated the city streets every night after dinner.

peremptory *(puh-REMP-tuh-ree), adjective*
Allowing for no rebuttal or overturning. A *peremptory* act is one that admits no possibility of denial or negotiation.

Kings may issue peremptory declarations of war, Mr. Secretary; presidents are obliged to discuss such matters with Congress.

perennial *(puh-REN-ee-ull), adjective*

Enduring. That which gives evidence of lasting indefinitely can be considered *perennial*. (Certain plants that have a long blooming cycle are called *perennials*.)

The nation's perennial budget crisis took an ugly new turn this week.

perfidy *(PURR-fih-dee), noun*

Treachery. *Perfidy* is a calculated breach of faith or trust.

In wartime, such perfidy as you have been found guilty of yields only one sentence: death.

perfunctory *(purr-FUNK-tuh-ree), adjective*

Mundane; routine. Also: showing little care. Something done with little interest is a *perfunctory* act.

Preoccupied, Tom went about his daily tasks with a perfunctory air.

perimeter *(puh-RIM-ih-tur), noun*

The outer edge of an enclosed shape or area. *Perimeter* can also refer to the distance described by this edge.

In the early morning hours Jake would take a walk along the perimeter of the yard.

peripatetic *(per-ih-puh-TET-ik), adjective*

Wandering. Someone who goes from one place to another is *peripatetic*.

These days, pursuing the presidency requires serious candidates to live a peripatetic lifestyle that profoundly affects one's home and family life.

periphery *(puh-RIFF-uh-ree), noun*

The area at the extreme of a given boundary. The outskirts of a town, for instance, are on the *periphery* of the town.

> *There among the homeless, at the furthest periphery of society, Maria found her calling.*

perjure *(PURR-jer), verb*

To lie or give false and misleading testimony. To *perjure* oneself is to commit the crime of testifying to something one knows is untrue.

> *Although Mr. Frattori was not convicted on the main charges he faced, he may serve time in prison for having perjured himself during the trial.*

permeate *(PURR-mee-ate), verb*

To penetrate. Something that *permeates* spreads throughout.

> *Joan's stories are permeated with a sense of spiritual mystery.*

pernicious *(purr-NISH-uss), adjective*

Tending to cause insidious harm or injury. *Pernicious* can also mean "fatal or likely to cause death."

> *A pernicious plague spread through the village.*

perpetuate *(purr-PETCH-oo-ate), verb*

To make everlasting; to prolong memory or use (of a thing). To *perpetuate* someone's memory is to cause that person's life to be recalled after his death.

> *The rumor that I am resigning has been perpetuated by a number of sources, all completely unreliable.*

persnickety *(purr-SNIK-uh-tee), adjective*

Fussy and overattentive to small details. *Persnickety* can also mean "snobbish."

> *Gordon made a point of being persnickety about meals: breakfast was always served in his home at exactly 7:04, and dinner at exactly 6:42.*

perspicacity *(per-spih-KASS-ih-tee), noun*
Insightfulness. Someone who shows keen understanding displays *perspicacity*.

> *The problem was a complex one that required the analysis of someone with great perspicacity.*

perspicuity *(purr-spi-KYOO-ih-tee), noun*
Clear and easy to understand. *Perspicuity* is generally used with regard to speech or writing.

> *The report from the accounting office was loaded with technical jargon; writing with perspicuity is not one of the talents of the people who work there.*

peruse *(puh-ROOZ), verb*
To read through with attention. *Peruse* can also mean "to examine with an eye to detail."

> *The witness perused the document for some time, then declared that it was not the one he had signed.*

pervasive *(purr-VAY-siv), adjective*
Having infiltrated or penetrated. A *pervasive* rumor is one that has been circulated widely.

> *The prejudice against handicapped persons is no longer as pervasive as in years past.*

petulant *(PET-yoo-lunt), adjective*
Impatiently peevish. Someone who shows great annoyance or irritation with minor problems could be said to be *petulant*.

> *He dismissed their questions with a petulant wave of the hand and quickly changed the subject.*

philander *(fi-LAN-der), verb*
To engage in amorous flirtations or exploits with someone who one cannot or does not intend to marry. *Philander* is used in reference to the sexual habits of men, not women.

> *These accusations of philandering, whether based in fact*

or not, have little to do with the question of whether the candidate will serve our state well in the United States Senate.

philanthropy *(fih-LAN-thruh-pee), noun*
Generosity or benevolence toward mankind. Someone who acts out of *philanthropy* is someone who commits resources to the betterment of his fellow man. (A philanthropist is one who bestows wealth on public institutions or people in need.)

Toward the end of his life, Andrew Carnegie was a model of philanthropy.

physiognomy *(fiz-ee-OG-nuh-mee), noun*
The human face (especially when regarded as a mirror of one's emotional state). *Physiognomy* is also the practice of determining a person's inclination or character from facial signals.

There was a noticeable change in Doris's physiognomy as Todd read her the news.

picayune *(PIK-uh-yoon), adjective*
Petty. Something that is trifling or unimportant is *picayune*.

Mr. Frankl apparently couldn't be bothered with such picayune concerns as what color shirt to wear.

picturesque *(PIK-chuh-resk), adjective*
Reminiscent of or suggesting a (painted) picture. A striking or unusually interesting scene can be considered *picturesque*.

The film's picturesque setting is not enough to make up for its scant plot.

piety *(PIE-uh-tee), noun*
Devotion; religious reverence. Someone who shows a marked inclination to worship God is said to show *piety*.

Joseph Smith--a man not noted for his piety--suddenly started attending religious services.

pinnacle *(PIN-uh-kul)*, *noun*
The topmost point. To reach the apex or highest point of
something is to reach its *pinnacle*.

> *Fred reached the pinnacle of his profession when he was
> named chairman of the history department.*

pique *(peek)*, *verb*
To injure a person's pride and thereby engender harsh feelings.
Someone who shows resentful irritation at a perceived slight
can be said to be *piqued*.

> *Marcia was piqued at not having been invited to the
> party.*

placate *(PLAY-kate)*, *verb*
To appease. Someone who concedes or yields in order to
avoid another's anger can be said to *placate* that person.

> *Although the company was unable to raise wages, it did
> make an effort to placate the union by extending the
> afternoon coffee break.*

placebo *(pluh-SEE-bo)*, *noun*
A medicine having no fixed medical purpose or healing
property given either to pacify a patient or, as a control
method, to test the effectiveness of another drug. A *placebo* is
administered as though it were a medication or drug, yet is
neutral from a medical standpoint.

> *Scientists are still uncertain as to exactly what causes
> the placebo effect, in which some patients taking a
> "fake" drug actually improve.*

placid *(PLAH-sid)*, *adjective*
Undisturbed; smooth. That which appears calm or undisturbed
on the surface can be said to be *placid*.

> *The placid country surroundings were just the change
> Caitlyn needed after three months in noisy Manhattan.*

plague *(playg), noun*
A broad-based affliction. A *plague* is a widespread calamity usually associated with a severe and sudden incidence of disease in a population. (*Plague* can refer to divine intervention or, figuratively, to any sudden and widespread reversal of fortune affecting a group: "a *plague* of bank closures.")

> *Fortunately, humans have not encountered a severe outbreak of the bubonic plague for centuries.*

platitude *(PLAT-ih-tood), noun*
A commonplace or useless remark. A statement that is trite or unoriginal can be considered a *platitude*.

> *You have taken a speech that seemed quite promising and filled it to the brim with platitudes.*

platonic *(pluh-TON-ik), adjective*
Free from sexual desire. *Platonic* also refers to the ideal form of something.

> *Emily knew that her relationship with Paul had to remain a platonic one.*

plaudit *(PLAW-dit), noun*
An expression of gratitude or praise. *Plaudits* (in the plural) is usually taken to mean "applause."

> *I am unworthy, my friends, of the plaudits you have bestowed on me this evening.*

plenitude *(PLEN-ti-tood), noun*
Abundance. *Plenitude* is the standard spelling; *plentitude*, though commonly used, is generally considered incorrect.

> *The sudden plenitude of supplies was certainly a welcome change for the hungry travelers.*

plethora *(PLETH-er-uh), noun*
Excessive oversupply. To have a *plethora* of something is to have a vast quantity of it.

The new edition contains a plethora of trivia concerning the films made by Mr. Howard and his cohorts in the forties and fifties.

pliant *(PLY-unt), adjective*

Supple. Something that is modified or altered easily is *pliant*.

You must mold papier mache quickly; it is not pliant for long.

plight *(plite), noun*

Predicament, especially one arising from a solemn obligation. A *plight* is an unfortunate or desperate situation.

Out of sympathy for the public television station's plight, Glenn made a large donation.

plutocracy *(ploo-TOK-ruh-see), noun*

Rule by the rich. *Plutocracy* can also refer to the overall influence of the wealthy in social affairs.

"If plutocracy were likely to improve the nation's standard of living," Gerald said haughtily, "then I would be a plutocrat."

poignant *(POY-nyunt), adjective*

Appealing to the emotions. That which is acutely painful or affecting is *poignant*.

The film's final scene is meant to be poignant, but I found it cloying.

polarize *(PO-luh-rize), verb*

To encourage elements or components to occupy opposite ends of a spectrum. Something that divides or sows discord is said to *polarize*.

The scandal left the two wings of the party completely polarized.

polemics *(puh-LEM-ik), noun*

The art of argument. Someone who is strong in the field of

polemics is gifted in making points by means of controversial discourse with others.

> *The talk show host's great asset was his skill in polemics--not his personality.*

polity *(POL-ih-tee), noun*
A system of government. A nation's *polity* is its structure of social and political functioning.

> *The polities of the Greek city-states, admired as they may be, cannot serve as a literal model for a modern industrial society.*

polyglot *(POL-ee-glot), noun*
A person who speaks a number of languages. Someone fluent in French, German, and English would be a *polyglot*.

> *The President's translator, a polyglot, served him well in missions to Germany, Portugal, and Mexico.*

pontificate *(pon-TIF-ih-kate), verb*
To issue authoritative decrees (as a pontiff might). *Pontificate* usually carries a sense of self-righteous pomposity.

> *Can I assume the Senator now intends to pontificate on the many virtues of our current trade policy?*

portend *(por-TEND), verb*
To suggest or foretell. If A *portends* B, A signifies that B is imminent.

> *The tone of Joan's voice this morning portends trouble.*

posit *(POZ-it), verb*

To stipulate. Someone who *posits* a thing presents or assumes it.

> *In his address, the mayor posited the conditions he would have to meet to resolve the fiscal crisis.*

potable *(POH-tuh-bull)*, *adjective*
Drinkable. Something that can be drunk safely is *potable*.

> *No amount of boiling could make the water from the stagnant lake potable.*

potentate *(POT-n-tate)*, *noun*
A powerful person. An influential political or business figure could be considered a *potentate*.

> *The First Lady was thoroughly at ease with foreign potentates and diplomats from the Administration's first day.*

pragmatic *(prag-MA-tik)*, *adjective*
Practical. Something that is *pragmatic* is useful or apt.

> *The Governor, in this case, decided not to take the advice of the ideologues, opting instead for a pragmatic approach.*

precarious *(pruh-KARE-ee-us)*, *adjective*
Insecure. Something that is *precarious* is uncertain and subject to misfortune or collapse.

> *The crisis has left our nation in a precarious position.*

precedent *(PRESS-i-dent)*, *noun*
A previous parallel incident justifying a present action. A *precedent* is an example from the past that is either identical to a current situation or similar enough to it to use as a guide.

> *There is no precedent for the action the defense is requesting, Your Honor.*

precipice *(PRESS-ih-pis)*, *noun*
A cliff. To be "on the *precipice*" can also be to be on the verge of a dangerous course of action.

> *Though the view is spectacular here, I don't advise walking near the precipice.*

precocious *(pri-KO-shuss), adjective*
Prematurely advanced, especially with regard to mental ability. A child who vies for attention by displaying adult-like social or mental skills is also said to be *precocious*.

> *Bill, a precocious nine-year-old, could already do algebra and geometry.*

preemptive *(pre-EMP-tive), adjective*
Possessing and acting on a prior right (for instance, as one who has the first claim to purchase a property.) Similarly, to take a *preemptive* action is to act before others can.

> *The old miner had a preemptive claim to the property, and so our purchase of it was impossible.*

presage *(PRESS-ij), verb*
To foretell or indicate. If A *presages* B, A serves as a warning or sign that B will occur soon.

> *Such provocation may presage armed conflict in the region.*

prescience *(PRESS-ee-unce), noun*
Foreknowledge. *Prescience* is the knowledge of events before they take place.

> *Lacking prescience, I really can't tell you what Sally intends to do.*

pretense *(PREE-tence), noun*
An instance of pretending. To make a *pretense* of surprise, for instance, is to falsely act or claim to be surprised.

> *We will prove here that the lease was signed under false pretenses.*

prevaricate *(pri-VARE-uh-kate), verb*
To avoid revealing the true nature of one's position, actions, feelings, etcetera. Someone who "waffles" on an issue, throwing up distractions or responding to questions evasively, is said to *prevaricate*.

My opponent has chosen to prevaricate rather than address his role in the scandal.

prima donna *(PREE-muh DON-nuh), noun*
A self-centered member of a group or organization who feels that his contributions are so important as to merit special treatment. (Literally, a *prima donna* is the leading female singer in an opera company.)

> *There is no place for prima donnas in this organization; we must work together as a team.*

primordial *(pry-MORE-dee-UL), adjective*
Original. Something that is *primordial* comes at the very first position in a sequence.

> *Perhaps science can't answer such primordial questions as "How did the universe begin?"*

pristine *(PRISS-teen), adjective*
Unspoiled; primitive. Something that is *pristine* is original and uncorrupted by later influence.

> *The pristine wilderness had an invigorating effect on Charles, who had never gone camping before.*

proclivity *(pro-KLIV-ih-tee), noun*
A predisposition. To have a *proclivity* to do something is to tend to do it.

> *Allen has a proclivity to untidiness that will not go over well with Ralph.*

procrustean *(pro-KRUS-tee-un), adjective*
Seeking to enforce doctrines or theories by violently eliminating all possible alternative viewpoints. *Procrustean* derives from the name of a fabled thief of ancient Greece who stretched or amputated his victims in order to make them fit a bed exactly.

> *The regime's procrustean tactics are designed to completely eliminate all political dissent.*

procure *(pro-KYOOR), verb*
To obtain. Someone who *procures* something gathers or collects it.

> *Susan soon procured sufficient financing to close the deal.*

prodigal *(PRAW-dig-ul), adjective*
Wasteful or extravagant. Due to the influence of the biblical parable of the Prodigal Son (who wanders abroad spending his inheritance frugally) *prodigal* is often taken to mean "traveling," but this is not the original sense.

> *Harry had always been prodigal with his greeting card mailings, sending cards to people he barely knew in the hopes of solidifying business contacts.*

prodigy *(PRAW-dih-gee), noun*
A person possessing extraordinary skill or talent. A *prodigy* can also be a wonder or marvelous example.

> *The young Mozart, a famous child prodigy, played the piano with the skill of a master.*

profligate *(PROFF-lih-git), adjective*
Shamelessly immoral. *Profligate* can also mean extravagantly or recklessly wasteful.

> *Cedric abandoned his profligate ways and decided it was time to live life along the straight and narrow.*

profundity *(pruh-FUN-dih-tee), noun*
Depth of reasoning or insight. Something that shows *profundity* gives evidence of great understanding and intellectual incisiveness.

> *A paper's length is no indication of its profundity.*

progenitor *(pro-JEN-ih-ter), noun*
An ancestor who can be traced back through the direct line. A *progenitor* can also be the originator of a school of thought or organization.

Picasso, considered by many the progenitor of Cubism, showed a mastery of conventional painting technique in his very early work.

prognosticate *(prog-NOSS-tih-kate), verb*
To predict. Someone who foretells the future *prognosticates*.

As to the game's final outcome, I refuse to prognosticate.

progressive *(pruh-GRESS-iv), adjective*
Forward-moving, especially with regard to socal or political issues. A *progressive* politician is one who is associated with reform movements or similar causes.

Governor Dowling's retirement is seen as a severe blow to the entire progressive movement.

proliferate *(pro-LIF-uh-rate), verb*
To multiply or come into being rapidly. To *proliferate* can also mean to spread or become more common at an accelerated pace.

After the film's success, a number of cheap imitations proliferated for a time.

prolix *(pro-LIKS), adjective*
Tediously wordy. Something that is long and verbose is *prolix*.

The report was utterly prolix; I gave up trying to finish reading it.

promiscuity *(prom-ih-SKYOO-ih-tee), noun*
Indiscriminate choice of sexual partners. A *promiscuity* can also be an instance of promiscuous sex.

The comparatively tolerant attitude toward the promiscuity of the late '70s and early '80s changed dramatically with the onset of the AIDS crisis.

promulgate *(PROM-ul-gate), verb*
To put forward publicly. To *promulgate* can also mean "to announce in an official capacity."

The news of the British attack was promulgated by town criers.

propagate *(PROP-uh-gate), verb*
To cause to multiply by natural processes. *Propagate* is related to the word propaganda, which means "that (information) which is disseminated for public circulation by a person or party for advantage."

Darwin's observations on the way species propagate and adapt were shocking to many readers.

propinquity *(pruh-PIN-kwih-tee), noun*
Nearness, especially with regard to place, sequence, or heredity. If A is in close proximity to B, A is in *propinquity* to B.

Living in propinquity to constant civil conflict, as I did, is hardly a recipe for a happy childhood.

propound *(pruh-POUND), verb*
To set forth. To *propound* is to offer (a theory) for review or consideration.

Dr. Richards propounded his most complex mathematical theory yet at the conference.

prosaic *(pro-ZAY-ik), adjective*
Commonplace or workaday. Something that is unromantic or matter-of-fact is *prosaic*.

Banks, whose prosaic outlook on life left little room for frivolity, was a stern father.

proscribe *(pro-SKRIBE), verb*
To prohibit. To *proscribe* is also to denounce as injurious.

Any discussion of the fleet's battle plan was proscribed under threat of imprisonment.

proselytize *(PROSS-uh-luh-tize), verb*
To attempt to convert to one's own religious faith. Someone who *proselytizes* attempts (often overbearingly) to recruit others

to his religion.

> *It is not my intention to proselytize, but rather to share some insights on my own experiences within the Jewish faith.*

protean *(PRO-tee-un), adjective*
Capable of taking many shapes. Something that is easily variable or changeable in form is *protean*.

> *The actress's protean ability to portray members of many nationalities never ceases to amaze me.*

protege *(PRO-tuh-zhay), noun*
Someone aided by another influential person. A *protege* is a person who is protected, encouraged, or helped (for instance, in career matters) by another of superior status or rank.

> *Everyone expected Dean to name Bill (his protege) to the new post.*

protocol *(PRO-tuh-call), noun*
Formal etiquette, especially as practiced in diplomatic circles. *Protocol* can also refer to established rankings followed in a social gathering.

> *Her inability to adhere to official protocol led to her dismissal from the embassy staff.*

prototype *(PRO-tuh-type), noun*
The original model of something. A *prototype* is the experimental or trial version of a system or invention.

> *The prototype underwent several modifications before Ben felt comfortable showing it to potential investors.*

proverbial *(pruh-VER-bee-ul), adjective*
Calling to mind (a familiar) proverb. Something that is *proverbial* shows an immediate parallel with a well-known saying, story, or maxim.

> *Stan considered his younger brother about as useful as*

the proverbial fifth wheel.

providence *(PROV-ih-dnce), noun*
Divine care. To trust in *providence* is to hold an assurance that God will provide for needs or guide one's actions. (*Providence* can also mean "thrift.")

> *Despite Mother's assurance that providence will see to our needs, I feel I should try to find a job.*

provocative *(pruh-VOK-uh-tive), adjective*
Stimulating or combative. Someone who is *provocative* tends to focus on controversial issues.

> *Despite Ed's provocative attitude--or perhaps because of it--he won the respect of his supervisor on the creative team.*

prudent *(PROOD-nt), adjective*
Exercising due care with regard to one's interests. Something that is *prudent* is judicious or carefully considered.

> *I believe the merger was a prudent course of action, one that will solidify our cash position immediately.*

prurient *(PROOR-ee-ent), adjective*
Lewd (said of an idea, representation, account, etcetera). A *prurient* interest is one focusing excessively on sex.

> *"The idea," Judge Cotlin wrote, "that Joyce's Ulysses is designed mainly to excite the reader's prurient interest is absurd."*

psychosomatic *(sy-ko-suh-MAH-tik), adjective*
Pertaining to disorders having emotional or mental (rather than evident physical) causes. *Psychosomatic* can also refer to that which involves both mind and body.

> *Although the first doctor she consulted insisted that Jane's symptoms were psychosomatic, the second found signs of physical illness.*

puerile *(PYOO-ur-ul)*, *adjective*
Juvenile. *Puerile* derives from a Latin word meaning "boyish."

> *Such puerile babbling is not fit to be printed in the Letters section of this newspaper.*

pugilism *(PYOO-juh-liz-um)*, *noun*
Boxing. *Pugilism* is the science or practice of fistfighting.

> *Finally, the two pugilists stepped into the ring; the match was about to begin.*

pugnacious *(pug-NAY-shuss)*, *adjective*
Prone to quarrels or fights. A *pugnacious* person is one who is given to conflict or dispute.

> *Aaron's pugnacious attitude is the reason he is involved in so many arguments.*

pulchritude *(PUL-kri-tood)*, *noun*
Beauty. *Pulchritude* is derived from the Latin word for "beautiful."

> *Grandpa, who is given to extravagant talk, sometimes called Grandma "pulchritude herself" with a twinkle in his eye.*

punctilious *(punk-TILL-ee-uss)*, *adjective*
Overly attentive to trifling details. Someone who takes great care to dispose of seemingly small matters in a formally correct way is *punctilious*.

> *The punctilious Mrs. Smith took issue with the seating arrangements we had suggested.*

puritanical *(pyoor-ih-TAN-ih-kull)*, *adjective*
Reminiscent of the Puritans (whose strict lifestyle took an extremely narrow view of what was morally acceptable). To issue or follow overly restrictive, moralistic standards about work or socializing is to be *puritanical*.

> *Faith took a rather puritanical outlook on the*

importance of working a full day; a simple cold was not going to stop her from showing up at work.

purlieus *(PURL-yooz)*, noun
Neighborhood. Also: outskirts. The word *purlieus* takes a plural verb.

> *The officer's beat extended through the city's seamier purlieus: the South of Market and Tenderloin districts.*

purported *(purr-POR-tid)*, adjective
Supposed. Something represented as being (but not actually) the case is *purported* to be true.

> *I saw little sign of the luxurious lifestyle Mr. Hall is purported to enjoy.*

putative *(PYOO-tuh-tive)*, adjective
Reputed or generally regarded by common assent. *Putative* is sometimes confused with punitive, which means "inflicting punishment."

> *The defendant, putative head of the city's most notorious crime family, entered the courtroom confidently.*

pyrrhic *(PEER-ik)*, adjective
Gained at an injustifiably high cost. A *pyrrhic* victory refers to the ancient King Pyrrhus of Epirus, who observed after a particularly bloody battle that another similar victory would destroy his kingdom.

> *You must admit that selling a great many products on which we will lose money would be something of a pyrrhic victory.*

quagmire *(KWAG-mire)*, noun
An entanglement that offers no ready solution or means of escape. Literally, a *quagmire* is a boggy patch of ground which wagons and caravans often cannot pass over.

> *The hostage situation, which once worked in the President's favor, now threatens to become the worst quagmire of his administration.*

qualm *(kwalm), noun*
A misgiving or pang of conscience (at one's course of action).
To have *qualms* about a particular action is to wonder whether
or not it is right.

> *He had no qualms about leaving his job; he had given
> the company three very good years.*

quark *(kwork), noun*
An elementary particle. A *quark* is one of the smallest known
quantities of matter.

> *Phillip's work in applied physics focused on the behavior
> of quarks in various environments.*

querulous *(KWER-uh-luss), adjective*
Given to complaining. Someone who makes peevish complaints
is *querulous*.

> *Adrienne, a querulous young woman, complained
> about all her problems during lunch hours at work.*

quintessence *(kwin-TESS-unce), noun*
A thing's highest or most sublime essential form. To be the
quintessence of a thing is to embody it as well as conceivably
possible.

> *Jacqueline was in my view the quintessence of charm
> and grace that evening.*

quixotic *(kwik-SOT-ik), adjective*
Hopelessly and impractically idealistic. *Quixotic* is derived from
the literary character Don Quixote, whose romantic view of the
world is at odds with the harsh realities of existence.

> *Arthur's quixotic search for financial backing for his get-
> rich-quick schemes only amused Betty.*

rabbinical *(ruh-BIN-ih-kul), adjective*
Of or pertaining to rabbis. Another acceptable form of
rabbinical is *rabbinic*.

I intend to take up rabbinical studies in September.

ramification *(ram-ih-fih-KAY-shun), noun*
Eventual consequence. *Ramification* is, literally, the process of extending along branchlike progressions; an act's ramifications, then, are the events or situations arising from it over time.

> *I believe the ramifications of approving this bill have not been thought through fully.*

rankle *(RANG-kul), verb*
To cause irritation or festering resentment. Someone who is peeved by a perceived slight or oversight is said to be *rankled*.

> *The criticism he recieved for his plan rankled Paul for some time.*

rapacious *(ruh-PAY-shuss), adjective*
Given to plunder or the forcible overpowering of another. *Rapacious* is related to the word rape.

> *The foe we face is a rapacious one who thinks nothing of overrunning the weak if it suits his purposes.*

rapport *(ruh-PORE), noun*
A favorable relationship or established pattern of communication. A *rapport* is characterized by mutual trust and understanding.

> *The assembly workers had developed a good rapport with the supervisor.*

rapprochement *(rap-rosh-MAWN), noun*
The repairing of damaged relations. To bring about a *rapprochement* is to improve an existing rift between two parties.

> *The process of rapprochement between the two countries was slow and laborious.*

rapture *(RAP-chur)*, *noun*
Ecstatic feeling. To experience *rapture* is to be carried into a realm of joy.

Beethoven's Ninth Symphony, well played, is enough to send me into fits of rapture.

rarefied *(RARE-uh-fied)*, *adjective*
Lofty or exalted. Something that is *rarefied* is refined and of high caliber.

I must admit I feel a little out of place in such rarefied company.

ratiocinate *(rash-ee-OSS-ih-nate)*, *verb*
To reason. To *ratiocinate* is to probe thoroughly by means of logical examination.

We have some of the best mathematical minds in the world working on this problem, and yet no one has proved able to ratiocinate with sufficient clarity to find a solution.

ravenous *(RAV-uh-nuss)*, *adjective*
Powerfully hungry. *Ravenous* can also mean intensely eager to be satisfied.

I am ravenous, but fortunately dinner will be served soon.

reapportionment *(re-uh-PORE-shun-ment)*, *noun*
Redistribution. *Reapportionment* is generally used with reference to changes in political districts based on shifting population.

The reapportionment of voting districts dramatically affected the balance of power in the House.

rebuff *(re-BUFF)*, *noun*
An instance of rejection or expressed disapproval. To receive a *rebuff* is to be sharply and summarily turned down.

> *Tim suffered his employer's rebuff shortly after proposing the new project.*

recalcitrant *(ri-KAL-sih-trunt)*, *adjective*
Resistant to authority. Someone who has difficulty working under any superior could be said to be *recalcitrant*.

> *Boot camp is not the best place for recalcitrant behavior, Mr.* Diamond.

recant *(rih-KANT)*, *verb*
To disavow (a formerly held view). Historically, people considered religious heretics have been forced to *recant* unauthorized beliefs by church authorities.

> *It was not until June that the Congressmen recanted and withdrew his support for the constitutional amendment.*

recapitulate *(re-kuh-PIT-yoo-late)*, *verb*
To summarize in concise form. To *recapitulate* a story is to relate its essential points briefly.

> *Sgt. Dennis, an eyewitness, recapitulated the incident to his superiors at headquarters.*

reciprocate *(re-SIP-ro-kate)*, *verb*
To give or act in turn following the lead of another. Someone who *reciprocates* reproduces the courtesy, gift, or example of another.

> *Mr. Powers has shown evidence that he wants to end the feud; the least you can do is reciprocate.*

reclusive *(ri-KLOO-siv)*, *adjective*
Hermitlike. Someone who shuts himself off from the influences of the world could be considered *reclusive*.

> *The reclusive millionaire lived the life of a hermit, never leaving his home.*

recompense *(REK-um-pense)*, *verb and noun*
To give compensation (for suffering or injury, for instance). As a noun, *recompense* means "that which is given in compensation."

> *There is no recompense for the loss you have suffered, Mrs. Williams.*

reconcile *(REK-un-sile)*, *verb*
To settle or bring into agreement. One can *reconcile* conflicts, contradictory columns of figures, or even internal emotions that seem at odds with each other.

> *How is the White House to reconcile these conflicting signals from the Kremlin?*

reconnaissance *(ri-KON-uh-sunce)*, *noun*
A search (of an area) made for the purpose of gaining information likely to yield military advantage. *Reconnaissaince* is borrowed from the French.

> *The pilot knew that a reconnaisance mission such as this one would be difficult and dangerous.*

reconnoiter *(rek-uh-NOY-ter)*, *verb*
To engage in reconnaisance. (See above.) *Reconnoiter* is from an old French verb meaning "to explore."

> *Your mission is to reconnoiter the area and meet back here at 0800 hours.*

rectify *(REK-tih-fie), verb*
To put right. Someone who *rectifies* a calculation corrects
the mathematical errors it contains.

> *Ellen rectified her previous mistakes and filed the
> report.*

recumbent *(ri-KUM-bent), adjective*
Lying down. *Recumbent* can also mean "inactive."

> *Oscar lay on the beach, recumbent beneath the warm
> Hawaiian sun.*

redundant *(rih-DUN-dunt), noun*
Superfluous. That which fulfills the role of something already
in place and functional is *redundant*.

> *Many of the functions of the shuttle vehicle are
> deliberately designed to be redundant in order to
> provide backup systems in case primary systems fail.*

refurbish *(re-FUR-bish), verb*
To renovate or repair. To *refurbish* is to restore to a state of
attractive completion.

> *The housing project's volunteers refurbished the
> abandoned apartments in record time.*

relentless *(ri-LENT-lis), adjective*
Unceasingly harsh. Something that is unyieldingly intense or
severe is *relentless*.

> *Under the relentless questioning of the prosecutor,
> Diane lost her composure.*

relevance *(REL-uh-vence), noun*
The quality of being pertinent. That which has a connection
or apt association has *relevance*.

These sales figures have no relevance for our purposes; they are at least six years old.

relinquish *(ri-LING-kwish), verb*
To give up. Someone who surrenders or forswears a thing *relinquishes* it.

> *The King relinquished his throne to marry the woman he loved.*

remunerate *(ri-MYOO-ne-rate), verb*
To pay (in consideration of another person's expense or action). To *remunerate* is to settle an existing financial obligation by means of payment.

> *The insurance company remunerated the accident victim only after months of delaying.*

renege *(ri-NEG), verb*
To go back (on one's word). Someone who breaks a promise or commitment *reneges* on an agreement.

> *Dalton was supposed to have been named vice president in exchange for his support, but Peterson reneged on the deal after assuming control.*

renounce *(re-NOWNCE), verb*
To abandon or deny any connection with. Someone who *renounces* something severs all ties to it.

> *Only by renouncing all desire for possessions, the monks believed, could one attain enlightenment.*

replete *(ri-PLEET), adjective*
Full. To say A is *replete* with B is to say A is supplied to the highest possible level with B.

> *The market was replete with everything the holiday shopper could have wanted.*

replicate *(REP-li-kate), verb*
To reproduce (an event or action). *Replicate* can also mean "to bend back."

> *Dr. Yate believed he had made an important discovery, but he was unable to replicate his experiment for the other scientists in his group.*

reprehensible *(rep-ri-HEN-sih-bull), adjective*
Abhorrent. That which is morally inexcusable is *reprehensible*.

> *I agree that the crimes were reprehensible; they were not, however, committed by my client.*

reprieve *(ri-PREEV), verb*
A suspension or delay from imminent proceedings. A *reprieve* is a respite.

> *The inmate won a last-minute reprieve from the Governor.*

reproach *(ri-PROACH), verb and noun*
To express stern disapproval of. As a noun, *reproach* means scornfully stated disdain.

> *Your many efforts to get on Harvey's good side have succeeded only in winning his reproach.*

reprobate *(REP-ruh-bate), noun*
An unprincipled person. A *reprobate* is someone who has crossed an accepted line describing morally sound behavior.

> *From that day on Johnson was considered a reprobate, and was shunned in the town.*

reprove *(re-PROOV), verb*
To censure. Someone who corrects or finds fault *reproves*.

> *Reproving children can only go so far; you must set a*

good example for them, as well.

repudiate *(rih-PYOO-dee-ate), verb*
To disprove and thereby render obsolete. A theory that has been *repudiated* is one that is accepted as invalid.

This survey totally repudiates the findings Geraldson claims in his earlier paper; his model can no longer stand.

repugnance *(ri-PUG-nunce), noun*
Disgust. To show strong aversion for something is to show *repugnance*.

We can greet the news of the terrorist bombing only with repugnance.

requisite *(REK-wi-zit), adjective*
Necessary. That which is required or essential is *requisite*.

Having failed to fill out the requisite forms, Lydia missed the opportunity to enter her work in the fair.

rescind *(ri-SIND), verb*
Reverse (for instance, an order, command, or edict). To *rescind* an instruction is to overrule it.

The order of detention is hereby rescinded; you may return to your native country at your earliest convenience, Mr. Dawson.

resilience *(ri-ZIL-yunce), noun*
The ability to rebound. That which bounces back shows *resilience*.

Joanne's resilience was remarkable; she recovered from the operation in record time.

resolute *(REZ-uh-loot)*, *adjective*
Unyielding in determination. Someone who is firm of purpose is *resolute*.

> *We remain resolute on the question of the hostages: they must be released without precondition.*

resonate *(REZ-uh-nate)*, *verb*
To vibrate or sound in a way similar to something else. In addition, that which matches or complements an existing pattern can be said to *resonate* with that pattern.

> *The sound of clicking footsteps resonated through the cavernous hallway.*

resplendent *(ri-SPLEN-dent)*, *adjective*
Brilliantly shining. That which is splendidly lustrous is *resplendent*.

> *A sky resplendent with stars awaited Norman and his telescope.*

restitution *(res-ti-TOO-shun)*, *noun*
The act of compensating for a past misdeed. To make *restitution* for something is to acknowledge to wrongness of a past act and attempt to repair the damage caused by it.

> *A bill authorizing restitution to the citizens interned in the camps recently cleared Congress.*

restive *(RES-tive)*, *adjective*
Uneasy; impatient with delay. Someone who is impatient or uncomfortable with present surroundings could be said to be *restive*.

> *The restive players gathered around the coach, eager to get the game underway.*

resurgence *(ri-SUR-jents), noun*
Reappearance or revival. Something that has a *resurgence* returns to a position of prominence or visibility.

> *A resurgence of popularity for bell-bottom slacks is not expected this season, but the experts have been wrong before.*

resurrect *(rez-uh-REKT), verb*
To bring back from the dead. Figuratively, to *resurrect* something (a fashion, for instance) is to reintroduce it after it has been dismissed as no longer relevant or appropriate.

> *It astounds me that you have gone to the trouble to resurrect these completely discredited ideas.*

reticent *(RET-ih-sent), adjective*
Reserved. Someone who prefers silence to conversation in social settings could be said to be *reticent*.

> *Little Amy was reticent at the party, staying close to her mother and avoiding all talk with strangers.*

retinue *(RET-n-oo), noun*
A group of companions or followers (of a person of great importance). A *retinue* is an entourage.

> *The President and his retinue are expected here just before noon.*

retribution *(ret-ruh-BYOO-shun), noun*
Punishment (as from God) for past wrongdoing. *Retribution* can also refer to divine reward for the just, but the negative sense is more common.

> *Some saw the mafia don's debilitating illness as a form of divine retribution for a life of crime.*

retroactive *(ret-ro-AK-tiv)*, *adjective*
Effective back to a stated point in time. Something that is made *retroactive* is extended as though it had been taking place since a certain past date.

> *We will be raising your salary to $100,000 a year, Perkins, retroactive to January 1.*

retrospect *(RET-ruh-spekt)*, *noun*
Hindsight. *Retrospect* derives from the Latin roots for "backward" and "vision."

> *In retrospect, the decision to launch the attack at night now seems like a catastrophic error.*

revamp *(re-VAMP)*, *verb*
To redo. To *revamp* is to renovate thoroughly.

> *The playwright decided to revamp several of the weaker scenes in the first act.*

revile *(rih-VILE)*, *verb*
To curse or abuse in harsh language. Someone who is *reviled* by another is denounced or hated by that person.

> *Realizing that he was reviled by those opposing his stand on the military buildup, the Senator decided to cancel his appearance at the campus.*

rhetoric *(RET-ur-ik)*, *noun*
The art of the effective use of language. *Rhetoric* is also speech or writing calculated to arouse passion.

> *Are we ever going to move from empty rhetoric to a sound plan of action on this issue?*

ribald *(RIB-uld)*, *adjective*
Amusingly coarse or lewd. A *ribald* story is one that is off-color.

*The young boys often retired to a spot behind the gym
where they would pretend to smoke cigarettes and
exchange ribald jokes none of them understood.*

rigmarole *(RIG-muh-role)*, noun

Nonsensically complicated procedure. *Rigmarole* is also
misleading and incomprehensible doubletalk.

> *I have had enough of this author's rigmarole; I want
> a book with some substance to it.*

rogue *(roag)*, noun

A scalawag. A *rogue* is a person (usually a man) known to
have low morals and habits.

> *Everyone in Savannah knew that Rhett was a rogue,
> but somehow he managed to use that fact to his
> advantage.*

rubicon *(ROO-bih-kon)*, noun

A point beyond which permanent change is unavoidable. The
word comes from the name of a river (the *Rubicon*) once
crossed by Julius Caesar in an act that led irrevocably to war.

> *In signing the bill, the Governor may have crossed the
> Rubicon and forever closed the door on his prison
> reform program.*

rudimentary *(roo-duh-MEN-tuh-ree)*, adjective

Basic. That which is elementary is *rudimentary*.

> *This thesis is full of rudimentary errors in grammar, to
> say nothing of several significant lapses in style.*

rueful *(ROO-ful)*, adjective

Regretful. Rueful can also mean *pitiable*.

> *In the terminal, Jean gave a rueful sigh as she stared
> at the plane that was to carry her away from*

San Francisco forever.

ruminate *(ROO-muh-nate), verb*
To ponder or review mentally. Someone who *ruminates* over something tosses it over in his mind.

> *Elaine was still ruminating over whether or not to attend college in the fall.*

rusticate *(RUSS-ti-kate), verb*
To move (a person) to the country. *Rusticate* can also mean "to accustom to country living."

> *I am afraid you will be unable to rusticate Ken; he is a city boy through and through.*

salacious *(suh-LAY-shuss), adjective*
Lewd or off-color. *Salacious* is generally used in reference to deliberately provocative pictures or writing.

> *Most magazines sent by family members to the troops were entirely innocent; who could find anything salacious in a copy of Golf Digest?*

salient *(SAY-lee-unt), adjective*
Relevant to the matter at hand. That which is *salient* has bearing on the current issue.

> *Grover Cleveland may very well have been elected to the White House twice, but the salient point is that in the year we are discussing, 1888, he was defeated by Benjamin Harrison.*

salivate *(SAL-ih-vate), verb*
To secrete saliva. To *salivate* over something is to eagerly anticipate eating it; the word has seen some figurative use in this sense.

> *We now know that dogs will salivate upon hearing a*

bell they associate with food, even if the food is not present.

salutary *(SAL-yoo-tare-ee), adjective*
Promoting physical soundness. That which is conducive to good health is *salutary*.

> *The medicine Dr. Catton gave to Mother seems to have had a salutary effect.*

sanguine *(SAN-gwinn), adjective*
Possessing a positive attitude. *Sanguine* usually carries the sense of being cheerful despite obstacles or potential problems.

> *Despite the many setbacks she had faced, Ellen remained sanguine.*

sardonic *(sar-DON-ik), adjective*
Bitter or sarcastic. That which is derisively scornful is *sardonic*.

> *Milton gave a sardonic laugh when asked if he would mind stepping aside to let someone else have a turn at the pinball machine.*

satiate *(SAY-shee-ate), verb*
Satisfy beyond reasonable expectation. To be *satiated* is to consume to excess.

> *If this Thanksgiving dinner doesn't satiate your appetite, nothing will.*

saturnine *(SAT-ur-neen), adjective*
Moody and morose. Someone who is *saturnine* is gloomy.

> *For some months after the death of his cat, Cosgrove maintained a saturnine front.*

savoir faire *(SAV-wahr FAIR)*, *noun*
An evident sense of confidence and proficiency. *Savoir faire* is a French phrase meaning "knowing how to do (it)."

> *Glen brought to the company a savoir faire about computers that no one else on the staff possessed.*

scapegoat *(SKAPE-goat)*, *noun*
A person considered responsible for a fiasco or mishap who was not in fact totally responsible for it. *Scapegoat* derives from an ancient practice of selecting a goat to accept the sins of a community.

> *I will not act as scapegoat in this affair; you all had a vote in the matter, and you all voted yes, just as I did.*

scathing *(SKAY-thing)*, *adjective*
Violently critical. *Scathing* usually refers to speech or writing about another's conduct or performance.

> *The scathing review by the* Times *theater critic had the anticipated effect: the show closed within two weeks.*

schematic *(skuh-MAT-ik)*, *adjective and noun*
Having to do with a diagram or scheme. As a noun, *schematic* can mean "a fully diagrammed plan or drawing."

> *Will you please refer to the schematic design I have reproduced on page twelve of your handbook?*

scintillate *(SIN-til-ate)*, *verb*
Giving off sparks. Something of remarkable interest that sets off a sudden reaction among people can also be said to *scintillate*.

> *News about the new film has been hard to come by, but a few scintillating details have leaked out.*

scrutinize *(SKROOT-n-ize), verb*
To review extremely closely. Someone who examines an object or document in minute detail *scrutinizes* it.

> *It is your job to scrutinize these applications carefully for any inaccuracies or misleading statements.*

seethe *(seethe), verb*
To boil. In addition, someone who internalizes agitation or anger can be said to *seethe*.

> *Still seething from his defeat at the hands of the Dodgers on Tuesday, Gibson took the mound with a look of unwavering determination last night.*

semantics *(suh-MAN-tiks), noun*
The science of the way meaning is communicated through language. A *semantic* distinction is one focused on the way something is phrased, rather than its underlying reality.

> *Whether we say the compensation will be "appropriate" or "competitive" is really a matter of semantics; we know exactly how much we intend to pay the person we finally hire.*

sententious *(sen-TEN-shuss), adjective*
Tending to use many cliches or maxims in order to enlighten others. Someone who shares many sayings or stories in a sanctimonious or preachy way is *sententious*.

> *Polonius's sententious manner of speaking clearly irritates Hamlet in this scene.*

septuagenarian *(sep-tuh-juh-NARE-ee-un), noun*
A person in his or her seventies. A *septuagenarian* is one who is between seventy and seventy-nine years old.

> *Grandmother, now 69, is not looking forward to becoming a septuagenarian.*

sequester *(si-KWES-ter), verb*
To set apart (from outside influence). That which is
protected from the prejudices of the external world is
sequestered.

> *The jury was sequestered, due to the extraordinary
> amount of publicity the trial generated.*

serendipity *(sare-un-DIP-ih-tee), noun*
The quality of coming upon important insights or discoveries
by accident. To experience *serendipity* is to encounter
fortunate coincidence.

> *It was pure serendipity that, nearly fainting with
> hunger, I came upon the stock of supplies that night.*

serpentine (SUR-pun-teen), adjective
Snakelike. That which is reminiscent of serpents is *serpentine*.

> *Most salespeople resent the stereotype of their
> profession as serpentine and ruthless.*

Shangri-La *(SHANG-gri LA), noun*
A paradise or utopia. *Shangri-La* is derived from the name a
fictional land of eternal youth encountered in the James
Hilton novel *The Lost Horizon*.

> *Stacey's first few days on the new job seemed like
> Shangri-La compared to the insanity of the position she
> had just left.*

shibboleth *(SHIB-uh-leth), noun*
A special term not widely known that, when used, identifies
the user as a member of a group. *Shibboleth* (a word with
biblical origins) can also refer to a peculiarity of fashion or
lifestyle common to a single group.

> *The more cynical in the department will tell you that
> career advancement has less to do with ability than
> with contacts and memorizing shibboleths.*

simile *(SIM-uh-lee), noun*
A comparison in speech or writing. "Her smile is like the morning sun" is an example of a *simile*.

By asking, "Shall I compare thee to a summer's day?" Shakespeare initiates a simile he will develop fully in succeeding lines of the sonnet.

similitude *(sih-MIL-ih-tood), noun*
Likeness or similarity. If A is a *similitude* of B, a is similar to B.

Bea and Rosa have a similitude of habits when it comes to cooking.

simulacrum *(sim-yuh-LAY-krum), noun*
An minor, unreal or eerie similarity. A *simulacrum* can also be an effigy.

The boy possessed only the barest simulacrum of the classic DeBerris brow, but something told me his claim to be a descendant was valid.

sine qua non *(SEE-nay kwa NON), noun*
An essential feature (of something). *Sine qua non* is Latin for "without which not."

Many people consider a happy ending to be the sine qua non *of a proper comedy.*

skittish *(SKIT-ish), adjective*
Nervous and lacking confidence. Someone who is uneasy about approaching a task can be said to be *skittish* about it.

Lisa is still a bit skittish about the computer, George; perhaps you can give her a hand.

smattering *(SMAT-er-ing), noun*
A little bit. A *smattering* is a small amount of something.

Dean picked up a smattering of Italian during his visit to Venice.

sobriety *(so-BREYE-uh-tee), noun*
Clear-headedness. *Sobriety* is generally used to signify freedom from the influence of alcoholic drink.

> *My guess is that W.C. Fields had as few moments of sobriety in real life as he had in the movies.*

sobriquet *(SO-bri-ket), noun*
Nickname. A *sobriquet* is a special name for someone.

> *Mel's sobriquet here at the club is "Slicer."*

sociometry *(so-see-OM-uh-tree), noun*
The determination of preference among members of distinct social groups. *Sociometry* can also refer to distinctions accountable to social differences.

> *What we found is that the brand's success or failure in a given area was due not mainly to income level, but to sociometry.*

solace *(SOL-uss), noun*
Consolation. To give *solace* is to sympathize with and console.

> *The fact that he had thrown three touchdowns was little solace to Jim: all he could think about was losing the game.*

solecism *(SOL-ih-siz-um), noun*
An act that breaks formal rules. *Solecism* is generally taken to mean "a transgression of established standards" (for instance, with regard to etiquette or writing.)

> *She told her husband not to worry, that forgetting a host's name was only a minor solecism and certainly*

nothing to be concerned about.

solicitous *(sub-LISS-ih-tuss), adjective*
Openly concerned or worried (about the condition of another). Someone who is attentively eager to help is *solicitous.*

> *Joan could not have been more solicitous to Peter while he was sick.*

soliloquy *(sub-LIL-uh-kwee), noun*
In drama, a speech given by a character when no one else is present on stage. A *soliloquy* can also be any discourse a person gives to himself, or an account of a person's interior thoughts.

> *Hamlet's third act soliloquy was delivered in a strange, choppy manner that I found most unsettling.*

solipsism *(SOL-ip-siz-um), noun*
The idea that one's own perceptions are the only meaningful reality. *Solipsism* was once used to describe a philosophical doctrine, but it has also been taken to mean "the practice of extreme self-centeredness."

> *To the store manager, bringing thirteen items to the twelve-items-only line at the supermarket was an example of unforgiveable solipsism.*

sophistry *(SOF-iss-tree), noun*
A seemingly convincing argument that is logically flawed. To accuse someone of *sophistry* is to say he is practicing sly doubletalk.

> *I believe this jury is too sophisticated to be taken in by the sophistries the defense has offered.*

sordid *(SORE-did), adjective*
Tawdry. That which is base or undignified is *sordid.*

Desmond brought everyone up to date on all the latest gossip, omitting not a single sordid detail.

sovereignty *(SOV-rin-tee), noun*
Power or legitimacy as a nation. A nation's *sovereignty* refers to its self-determination and right to exist as a separate, independent entity.

The border incursion should be accepted for what it is: an affront against the sovereignty of our country.

spinster *(SPIN-ster), noun*
A single woman, especially a middle-aged one. *Spinster* usually carries negative connotations of unattractiveness and being past one's prime; there is no parallel expression that carries the same sense about an unmarried man.

Although Charles had expected a gathering of spinsters at the club meeting, he was greeted at the door by none other than the starting quarterback for the local college football team.

sporadic *(spo-RAD-ik), adjective*
Irregular. That which occurs at unpredictable intervals is *sporadic*.

Sporadic gunfire echoed down the streets all night.

spurious *(spyoor-ee-uss), adjective*
Inauthentic. *Something* that is not genuine is spurious.

There were many in the academic community who were ready to accept the spurious manuscripts as coming from Shakespeare's own hand.

stalemate *(STALE-mate), noun*
Literally, a position in a chess game in which there is no winner, yet neither side can make a legal move. *Stalemate* is often used to refer to a deadlocked political or military

situation.

> *Although the war had been waged for over three years,*
> *all the generals had to show for it was a bloody*
> *stalemate.*

stalwart *(STOL-wert), adjective*
Firm of purpose; steadfast. *Stalwart* can also mean
courageous.

> *Because the flight had been delayed by more than ten*
> *hours, only the most stalwart fans stayed up to greet*
> *the rock group at the airport.*

stereotype *(STAIR-ee-o-type), noun and verb*
A commonly accepted notion that presents an oversimplified
or inaccurate viewpoint (of a racial group's behavior, for
instance). As a verb, to *stereotype* someone is to assign him
characteristics in keeping with a popular image of the group
he belongs to, whether or not he possesses those
characteristics.

> *Most salespeople resent the stereotype of their*
> *profession as serpentine and ruthless.*

stigma *(STIG-muh), noun*
A sign of disgrace or low status. *Stigma* derives from a Greek
word meaning "tattoo;" presumably the sense of disgrace
arose from the practice of physically marking someone to
distinguish him as belonging to a lower class.

> *I was unprepared to deal with the social stigma of*
> *bankruptcy, yet it seemed my only available course of*
> *action.*

stipulation *(stip-yoo-LAY-shun), noun*
A condition. A *stipulation* is an essential point (of an
agreement or arrangement) that must be satisfied.

> *The will does feature one important stipulation: you*

must wait until you are thirty years old to receive the money.

stoic *(STO-ik).*
Above succumbing to sensations of pain or pleasure. *Stoic* originally referred to a philosophy that advocated putting aside unjust thoughts and indulgences and attending first and foremost to the duties of life.

Paul remained stoic when given the news that his father had finally succumbed to the illness.

strident *(STRY-dnt), adjective*
Harsh. Speech that is obtrusively grating is *strident*.

Dennis's appeals for money became more common--and more strident--as the year wore on.

stringent *(STRIN-jent), adjective*
Extremely strict. Regulations that leave little room for discretion are *stringent*.

The rules at the county swimming pool are quite stringent: only local residents are permitted to use the facility, and all the swimmers are required to wear bathing caps.

stultify *(STUL-tih-fy), verb*
To render foolish or unable to act intelligently. That which *stultifies* causes a decrease in mental power.

The intense heat had a stultifying effect on Melanie; she found she had difficulty thinking clearly.

stymie (STY-mee), verb
To stand in the way of or hinder. If A *stymies* B, A acts as an obstacle to B.

The other team's attempt to score was stymied when

we turned a double play with the bases loaded.

subjective *(sub-JEK-tiv), adjective*
Originating in one's personal observation. To say that
something is *subjective* is to say that it may be influenced
individual prejudice and represents only a particular person's
viewpoint.

> *Mind you, this is only a subjective observation, but my
> feeling is that that restaurant serves the worst Chinese
> food in the city.*

subjugate *(SUB-juh-gate), verb*
To cause to become subservient. To *subjugate* another is to
make him perform your will.

> *The dictator's attempts to subjugate his country's
> smaller neighbors will end in failure, mark my words.*

sublimate *(SUB-lih-mate), verb*
To transfer the force of an unacceptable inclination or
impulse to a pursuit considered proper. To *sublimate* an
urge is to redirect it to a wholesome purpose.

> *There is a popular--but unproven--notion that butchers
> are secretly violent, and that they choose their
> profession as a means of sublimating their passions.*

sublime *(suh-BLYME), adjective*
Grand or lofty. That which is splendid is *sublime.*

> *Many people can make a pretty good pot of spaghetti;
> mine, however, is sublime.*

subservient *(sub-SER-vee-unt), adjective*
Bending to the will of another. Someone who is *subservient*
is servile.

> *Stan always became meek and subservient in*

his boss's presence.

sully *(SUL-ee), verb*
To besmear or make foul. Figuratively speaking, to *sully* a person, group, or institution is to cast aspersions on it.

>*I will not allow you to sully the good name of my family with such baseless accusations.*

sumptuous *(SUMP-choo-us), adjective*
Extravagant. That which is lavish is *sumptuous*.

>*A sumptuous feast awaited the couple at the hotel.*

sundry *(SUN-dree), adjective*
Various. *Sundry* can also mean "an unspecified number more than two."

>*Sundry inexpensive plastic items were spread out on a table at the front of the store.*

supercilious *(soo-per-SIL-ee-uss), adjective*
Disdainful or haughty. Someone who is overbearingly proud could be said to be *supercilious*.

>*Randy can take on a supercilious air at times; you mustn't let his highminded behavior bother you.*

superfluous *(soo-PER-floo-uss), adjective*
Unnecessary. That which exceeds what is essential is *superfluous*.

>*The film's long production number was eventually cut from the final version because test audiences felt it was superfluous to the main plot.*

superlative *(soo-PER-luh-tiv), adjective*
To the highest possible degree. Something that is *superlative* is of surpassing quality or power.

Boris's superlative skills as a chess player are well known around campus.

supersede *(soo-per-SEED), verb*
To supplant or replace. If A now fulfills the function of B and makes B obsolete, A *supersedes* B.

This form, which supersedes the old version, has been made much easier to read and fill out.

supine *(SOO-pine), adjective*
Lying down with the back to the floor. *Supine* can also mean "passive."

Damon found the marketing department supine when it came to implementing ideas.

surcease *(sur-SEESE), noun*
End. A *surcease* is a cessation.

It was only with the surcease of hostilities that life began to return to normal for the region's civilian population.

surfeit *(SUR-fit), noun and verb*
Excess. To have a *surfeit* of something is to have too much of it.

We have had a surfeit of proposals and analysis; the time has come for us to act.

surrealistic *(suh-ree-uh-LISS-tik), adjective*
Unreal. *Surrealistic* art focuses on images or emotions that are otherworldly or profoundly removed from everyday experience.

The astronauts made their way across the surrealistic landscape of Mars.

surreptitious *(sur-up-TISH-uss), adjective*
Undertaken in stealth. That which is done in hiding is
done *surreptitiously*.

> *I have reason to believe our conference room has
> been fitted with "bugs" designed to monitor our
> conversations surreptitiously.*

surrogate *(SUR-uh-gut), noun*
One who acts in the place of another. *Surrogate* is
derived from a Latin verb meaning "to nominate in one's
place."

> *Although he was not related to Eric, Dean found
> himself acting as a surrogate brother to him.*

sycophant *(SIK-uh-funt), noun*
An ambitious flatterer. A *sycophant* is a person who tries
to improve his status by means of constant fawning
toward those in authority.

> *Presidents are usually surrounded by sycophants,
> but Lincoln found himself surrounded by potential
> political rivals.*

syllogism *(SIL-uh-jiz-um), noun*
A form of logical argument that features three propositions
and finishes with a conclusion. An example of a *syllogism*
would be "All elected Republican officials will be at the
meeting; all the members of Congress from my state are
elected Republican officials; therefore all the members of
Congress from my state will be at the meeting."

> *Aristotle's formulation of the syllogism as a tool
> for logical analysis is one of the most significant
> contributions to Western thought.*

symbiotic *(sim-bee-OT-ik), adjective*
The quality of two dissimilar organisms living in the same
place in a mutually beneficial relationship. While *symbiotic*

is a word originating in the world of biology, it has been expanded to refer to certain mutually beneficial human relationships.

> *The two neighboring businesses found that their customer base overlapped, and that by recommending each other to visitors they could establish a mutually beneficial symbiotic relationship.*

symmetry *(SIM-ih-tree), noun*
The quality of showing complementary forms or aesthetically pleasing proportions. *Symmetry* is structural balance.

> *The sculpture's lack of symmetry is unnerving to the casual observer, and that is exactly what the artist has in mind.*

synonym *(SIN-uh-nim), noun*
A word equivalent in meaning to another word. "Innocent" and "guiltless," for instance, are *synonyms.*

> *I have to come up with a synonym for "intelligent"; I've used that word three times in this paragraph.*

synopsis *(sih-NOP-sis), noun*
A summary. A *synopsis* is a brief recounting of the principle points of something.

> *A full synopsis of the play's plot would give away a delightful surprise ending, so I will not attempt one here.*

taciturn *(TASS-ih-turn), adjective*
Quiet. Someone who tends to avoid speech is *taciturn.*

> *You must understand that Betty can be quite taciturn after a day at work; her silence is not*

because of anything you have done.

tactile *(TAK-tull)*, adjective
Of or pertaining to the sense of touch. That which relates to touching is *tactile*.

> *The infant's tactile development is especially rapid during this stage.*

tandem *(TAN-dum)*, adjective
One after another. To walk in *tandem* is to walk in single file.

> *We gave Mom and Dad a tandem bicycle for Christmas this year.*

tangible *(TAN-juh-bull)*, adjective
Real; touchable. That which exists corporeally is *tangible*.

> *The prosecution has offered many theories and speculations, but no tangible evidence linking my client to the murder.*

tantamount *(TAN-tuh-mount)*, adjective
Equivalent to in all meaningful respects. *Tantamount* derives from an old verb meaning "to amount to as much."

> *Please remember that, since this is a tight race, a vote for the third-party candidate is tantamount to a vote for my opponent.*

taurine *(TAW-rine)*, adjective
Of or pertaining to bulls. *Taurine* can also refer to the zodiacal sign Taurus.

> *Brian could display a certain taurine tenacity when it came to completing a project on time.*

tautology *(taw-TOL-uh-gee), noun*
Unnecessary repetition--in different words--of an already
stated idea. To describe someone as an "wealthy member
of the city's upper class" would be a *tautology*.

> *Your description of Brian as a "foreign illegal
> alien" is a tautology: every illegal alien is a
> foreigner.*

taxonomy *(tak-SON-uh-mee), noun*
The science of formal classification and naming. In
biology, *taxonomy* also has a more formal meaning related
to the classification of organisms.

> *The newly discovered insect was dubbed "Liliput"
> by the researchers, although its formal name was
> a question of taxonomy that no one felt hurried
> to resolve.*

technocracy *(tek-NOK-ruh-see), noun*
Government by engineers, technicians, or other highly
skilled members of society. *Technocracy* (a theory
popularized in the 1930s) gave us the word technocrat,
which refers to a person skilled in (economic or
managerial) technique who holds a position of power and
influence.

> *The claim that I would institute some sort of
> technocracy simply because I am a skilled
> manager ignores my years of service as a District
> Attorney.*

teetotaler *(tee-TOE-tuh-ler), noun*
Someone who does not drink alcohol under any
circumstances. *Teetotaler* was formed from the verb
teetotal, coined during the Temperance movement of the
19th century.

> *No wine for me, thanks; I've been a teetotaler
> since high school.*

telekinesis *(tel-uh-kuh-NEE-siss), noun*
The supposed ability to move objects by means of mental energy. *Telekinesis* derives from the Greek roots for "from a distance" and "movement."

> *Uri Geller's claim to possess powers of telekinesis has been thoroughly discredited.*

telepathy *(tuh-LEP-uh-thea), noun*
The supposed ability to read minds or communicate mentally. *Telepathy* is a form of ESP (extrasensory perception).

> *I hope you're not suggesting that I cheated on the exam by using telepathy.*

teleprompter *(TEL-uh-promp-tur), noun*
An automated means of displaying lines to be read by actors. The *teleprompter* is a device used in place of cue cards.

> *The show's most amusing moment--the failure of the teleprompter that forced actors to improvise-- had nothing to do with its script.*

temblor *(TEM-blor), noun*
An earthquake. *Temblor* is derived from a Spanish verb meaning "to quake."

> *Because residents had considered earthquakes unlikely to occur in the region, few structures had been built to withstand a major temblor.*

temerity *(tuh-MARE-uh-tee), noun*
Rashness; reckless disregard of danger or unpleasant consequences. To take a bold action is to show *temerity*.

> *You have the temerity to ask for a raise after showing up late forty percent of the time over the last three months?*

tenable *(TEN-uh-bull)*, *adjective*
Capable of being maintained. That which is *tenable* can be held.

> *The general warned the mayor that the troops' position was no longer tenable, and that preparations should be made to evacuate the city immediately.*

tenacious *(tuh-NAY-shuss)*, *adjective*
Unyielding; stubborn. Someone who is *tenacious* is hard put to give up.

> *Bill was a tough campaigner who put up a tenacious fight for the nomination, but in the end he came up short.*

tenet *(TEN-ut)*, *noun*
A principle. Something held to be true, valid, or essential by a group or organization is a *tenet*.

> *I think you will agree with me that the primary tenet of this company is that the customer must come first.*

tenuous *(TEN-yoo-uss)*, *adjective*
Not solid (in terms of logical connection); insubstantial. Literally, *tenuous* means "slender (as a thread)."

> *The connection between the performance of the stock market and the result of the yearly Super Bowl game might seem tenuous at best, but there is evidence of some strange correlation between the two.*

tenure *(TEN-yur)*, *noun*
The holding of a post or property, especially with regard to status as a permanent employee. *Tenure* can also refer the period such a post is held.

After sixteen years in the department, Professor Milligan was finally granted tenure.

terra cotta *(tare-uh KOT-uh), noun and adjective*
A reddish clay modeling compound that hardens when exposed to extreme heat. *Terra cotta* is used primarily for pottery, the exterior facings of buildings, and sculpture.

> *The exhibition is notable for several gorgeous terra cotta sculptures of birds dating from the 1890's.*

tertiary *(TUR-shee-are-ee), adjective*
Third in succession. That which follows the second item in a list, sequence, or progression is *tertiary*.

> *The disease had progressed beyond its first two phases, and even showed signs of worsening beyond the tertiary stage.*

testator *(TESS-tay-tur), noun*
A male who sets out his wishes in a legal will. The female form of *testator* is *testatrix*.

> *The testator, I'm afraid, made a serious mistake in failing to have the will witnessed.*

testatrix *(tess-TAY-triks), noun*
A female who sets out her wishes in a legal will. The male form of *testatrix* is *testator*.

> *Let's keep one thing in mind: Mother is the testatrix, not you two, and she can dispose of her property in any way she sees fit.*

tete-a-tete *(TET ah tet), noun*
A meeting in which two people meet face-to-face. *Tete-a-tete* is French for "head-to-head."

> *You and Millie have done enough talking behind*

each other's back; I think the time has come for you to have a tete-a-tete and work this problem out once and for all.

Tetragrammaton *(tet-ruh-GRAM-uh-ton)*, noun
The written Hebrew word for God consisting of the four letters yod, he, vav, and he, and usually rendered *YHVH.* *Tetragrammaton* is Greek for "having four letters."

> *The sight of the Tetragrammaton carved in stone above the altar always filled Paul with a sense of inner peace.*

theocentric *(the-oh-SEN-trik)*, adjective
Placing God at the center (of a system of beliefs). That which focuses on God is *theocentric.*

> *You'll find this writer's philosophies a little more theocentric than the last one we studied.*

theocracy *(thee-OK-ruh-see)*, noun
Government by religious leaders. *Theocracy* is the concentrationof political power in the hands of church figures.

> *It was to prevent the excesses of theocracy (or its cousin, government by divine right) that the Founding Fathers forbade establishment of a formal state religion.*

therapeutic *(thare-uh-PYOO-tik)*, adjective
Having to do with cures for illness. That which is remedial is *therapeutic.*

> *The problem is not physical illness, but stress; I think you will find that a weekend in the country will have a strong therapeutic effect.*

thespian *(THESS-pee-un), noun*
An actor. *Thespian* refers especially to a person who
performs onstage in a play.

> *Sir Laurence Olivier was rightly regarded as the
> most versatile thespian of his era.*

tintinnabulation *(tin-tin-ab-yoo-LAY-shun), noun*
The ringing of bells. *Tintinnabulation* derives from a Latin
word meaning "bell."

> *The tintinnabulation from the center of the village
> left no one in doubt: Christmas had come at last.*

tirade *(TIE-raid), noun*
An extended outburst of harsh talk. Someone who delivers
a *tirade* gives a lengthy, overblown speech.

> *I did not come here to listen to a tirade about
> how inconsiderate my son is in class.*

titillate *(TIT-ih-late), verb*
To arouse or excite in a pleasing way. Something that
titillates tickles one's fancy.

> *These stories about the sex lives of past presidents
> may be titillating, but they wouldn't have passed
> for hard news in my day.*

titular *(TICH-uh-lur), adjective*
By title only. The *titular* head of a group is a person
who is technically designated as the leader, but who lacks
real power.

> *Ed may be the titular head of the organization,
> but I have a feeling that Bill has more influence
> in day-to-day matters.*

tome *(toam), noun*
A thick or heavy book. *Tome* applies especially to long, academically-oriented books.

> *I had been hoping to read something light that I could finish over my vacation, not a tome like this.*

toothsome *(TOOTH-sum), adjective*
Pleasant or appealing (especially with regard to taste.) *Toothsome* can also mean "alluring."

> *We concluded the feast with a toothsome banana split.*

torrential *(to-REN-shul), adjective*
Reminiscent of or pertaining to severe storms. That which is intense or unyieldingly powerful is *torrential*.

> *A torrential rain kept the children inside all day.*

torpor *(TOR-pur), noun*
Indifference, sloth or inactivity. *Torpor* is a state calling to mind the hibernation of animals.

> *Gregg's torpor on the job has been troubling me; I can't help wondering if he may be having trouble at home.*

tort *(tort), noun*
In law, a civil misdeed requiring compensation. *Tort* is a legal term sometimes misspelled as torte (see below.)

> *You are incorrect in assuming this would be a criminal case; we are looking at a tort, not a crime.*

torte *(tort), noun*
A cake made with eggs and very little flour. A *torte* has nothing to do with a tort (see above.)

Mrs. Carrigan's Linzer tortes are the best I have ever tasted.

tractable (TRAK-tuh-bull), adjective
Manageable or easy to control. Someone who takes instruction or guidance easily is *tractable.*

Jane was a willful and disobedient little girl, but her sister Annie was more tractable.

trajectory (truh-JEK-tuh-ree), noun
The path of flight followed by a projectile. A rocket's *trajectory* is the course it follows after takeoff.

The bullet's trajectory was a matter of some controversy in the case.

transcendental (tran-sun-DEN-tl), adjective
Beyond the realm of normal experience or understanding. That which transcends our customary bounds of perception is *transcendental.*

While the astronauts reacted in different ways to the transcendent experience of space travel, all were profoundly affected by the experience.

transgression (trans-GRESH-un), noun
A violation of a rule. To break a law or guideline is to commit a *transgression.*

David was perhaps a little too eager to cross over into Mr. Peterson's yard to play ball, but this was a minor transgression.

translucent (tranz-LOO-sunt), adjective
Capable of allowing some light to show through, but not transparent. A gauzy shower curtain, for instance, is *translucent.*

From my bed, through the translucent hospital curtains, I could dimly make out that a scuffle of some kind was taking place in front of the building.

transpire *(tran-SPIRE), verb*
To take place. That which happens *transpires*.

Mrs. Potter, please tell the court exactly what transpired that night as you remember it.

transpose *(trans-POZE), verb*
To reverse or change the position of. To *transpose* A and B is to put A in B's place, and vice versa.

The two frames of the film had been mysteriously transposed, so that it now looked as though the man's head moved forward suddenly instead of backwards.

travail *(truh-VALE), noun*
Hard work, especially work causing physical pain. *Travail* is sometimes used to describe the labor of childbirth.

It is not surprising that, given the travails of the long journey westward, some settlers opted to return East rather than try to make a life on the frontier.

travesty *(TRAV-ih-stee), noun*
A grotesque parody (of something). That which presents an insulting mockery (of a cherished institution, for instance) is a *travesty*.

Let's face it: the way Congress deals with overexpenditure is a travesty of its own budget reduction legislation.

treatise *(TREE-tiss), noun*
A scholarly essay or written argument. A systematic written examination of a subject is a *treatise*.

Mill's treatise on the equality of women was revolutionary for its time.

trenchant *(TREN-chunt), adjective*
Cutting or keen. That which is incisive is *trenchant*.

Bill's trenchant wit is out of place in such a stodgy organization.

trepidation *(trep-ih-DAY-shun), noun*
A state of fear or agitation. To have an apprehension is to have a *trepidation*.

At first, I approached the task of writing this book with some trepidation.

triennial *(tri-EN-ee-ul), adjective*
Ocurring every three years. That which occurs once in a three-year cycle is *triennial*.

The triennial Shakespeare festival takes place in April of every third year.

trifling *(TRY-fling), adjective*
Insignificant. That which is unimportant is *trifling*.

The fact is, you are unlikely to be called in for an audit over such a trifling amount of money.

troglodyte *(TROG-luh-dyte), noun*
One who behaves in a beastly, savage, or primitive manner. Literally, a *troglodyte* is a cave-dweller.

I knew that Sebastian would be uncommunicative after his ordeal, but I did not expect him to act like such a troglodyte at work.

truncheon *(TRUN-chun), noun*
A stick carried by police officers. A *truncheon* is a billy club.

The sight of the policemen beating the young demonstrators with truncheons, when beamed to the nation on television, was more than enough to ruin the convention for the party.

tryst *(trist), noun*

A prearranged meeting, especially one between lovers. *Tryst* derives from an old verb meaning "to make an arrangement with."

We've decided to celebrate our second honeymoon with a weekend tryst at the Ambassador Hotel.

tumultuous *(too-MUL-choo-uss), adjective*

Chaotic, especially as a result of a popular outcry. That which is in a violent uproar is *tumultuous*.

After the Board of Trustees rejected the students' proposal, there were tumultuous protests on campus.

tutelage *(TOOT-l-ij), noun*

The act of providing guided instruction or protection. *Tutelage* can also mean "close instruction."

It was under Dr. Clay's tutelage that he came to understand how much craft was required to write a solid play.

ubiquitous *(yoo-BIK-wi-tuss), adjective*

Seemingly everywhere at once. That which is *ubiquitous* is so common as to appear to be all places.

By the early '50s, that ubiquitous symbol of independence, the automobile, had influenced virtually every facet of American life.

ulterior *(ul-TIR-ee-ur), adjective*

Secret (especially of a purpose or motive). An *ulterior* purpose is one hidden from the outside world.

No one is suggesting that any ulterior motives came into play on Michael's part; all parties agree that he made a simple accounting error.

ultimatum *(ul-tih-MAY-tum), noun*
One's last set of demands. To issue an *ultimatum* is to outline a set of terms that cannot be compromised.

Either pay the rent by midnight on the thirty-first, or be thrown out in the street: that was Simon's ultimatum.

umbrage *(UM-brij), noun*
Resentful annoyance. To take *umbrage* is to express irritation.

I take umbrage at the suggestion that I have used my position here for illicit personal gain.

undulate *(UN-dyoo-late), verb*
Move in a wavelike motion. That which *undulates* moves in regular wavy patterns.

After a hard day at work, Ellis would sit on the seashore stare ahead at the undulating ocean to ease his mind.

unilateral *(yoo-ni-LAT-ur-el), adjective*
Undertaken independently, although likely to have implications for others (for instance, allies, associates, or family members). A *unilateral* decision is one made with no consultation of affected parties.

The allies resolved that no member country would take any unilateral act that might threaten mutual security.

upbraid *(up-BRAID), verb*
To criticize and assign blame (to a person). To *upbraid* is

to scold.

> *I did not spend thirteen years at this firm to be upbraided by a junior clerk, Mr. Franklin.*

upstage *(up-STAYJ)*, verb

To distract attention from (a person undertaking an act supposedly of primary interest). To *upstage*, in the theatrical sense, is to stand behind the main action of a scene and distract the audience.

> *I am not accustomed to being upstaged during a presentation, Peter.*

ursine *(UR-sin)*, adjective

Bearlike. *Ursine* derives from the Latin word for "bear."

> *Mr. Hess was so glad to see me that he ran across the hall and gave me a fierce (I might say ursine!) embrace.*

usurp *(yoo-SURP)*, verb

To assume forcibly and/or without right. To *usurp* is to take over.

> *The authority of Congress was indeed usurped by Lincoln during the war, but legislators briskly reasserted themselves once the crisis was past.*

usury *(YOO-sur-ee)*, noun

Excessive interest on a loan. Someone who demands extravagant payment in exchange for money lent out practices *usury*.

> *The rates you are charging for this loan you consider "fair," sir, border on usury.*

utilitarian *(yoo-til-ih-TARE-ee-un)*, adjective

Characterized by a concern for the practical or useful. That which is utilitarian is *pragmatic.*

> *I propose we take a utilitarian approach to the problem: since it no longer runs, why not scrap the old car completely and sell it for parts?*

utopia *(yoo-TOE-pee-uh)*, noun

A (theoretical) perfect society or paradise. *Utopia* was coined by using Greek forms to produce a word meaning "nowhere."

> *Any notion that granting eighteen-year-olds the right to vote would turn the country into a pastoral, strife-free utopia was quickly disproven.*

vacillate *(VAS-uh-late)*, verb

To waver between options. A person who cannot decide which course of action to settle on *vacillates.*

> *Mr. Mears's principal weakness is that he is seen as a vacillating leader, one who cannot choose one path and stick to it.*

vacuous *(VAK-yoo-uss)*, adjective

Lacking content or substance. That which is empty is *vacuous.*

> *Televised debates are so potentially dangerous that most candidates settle for offering vacuous recitations of campaign speeches rather saying something new and unexpected.*

vagary *(VAY-guh-ree)*, noun

An unexpected or seemingly capricious turn of events. A development that is unpredictable or (apparently) motivated by an impulsive arbitrariness is a *vagary.*

> *The vagaries of New England weather have undone many a planned excursion.*

vanguard *(VAN-gard)*, *noun*
The most advanced groups (of a military force or social movement, for instance.) That which is at the forefront is in the *vanguard*.

> *Dali was the first to admit that he took full financial advantage of his position at the vanguard of the Surrealist movement.*

variegated *(VAR-ee-uh-gay-tid)*, *adjective*
Changing in color. That which alters hue is *variegated*.

> *June's latest needlework project uses variegated thread to achieve a rainbow effect.*

vehement *(VEE-uh-ment)*, *adjective*
Strongly felt or marked by high emotion. That which is forceful and emphatic is *vehement*.

> *Congress overrode the President's veto after many members had openly expressed their vehement dissatisfaction with Administration policy.*

venerable *(VEN-er-uh-bull)*, *adjective*
Dignified and worthy of admiration. *Venerable* is often used to describe someone whose lifetime of achievement serves as a model example and commands unquestioned respect.

> *Stilling is not one to sit on his laurels; the venerable actor proves in his latest film that he still has the magic touch.*

verbiage *(VER-bee-uj)*, *noun*
Unnecessary words. Superfluous or overwrought language is *verbiage*.

> *Like many novelists, Robert overwrote: he would let everything fly in one session and then come back and pare away at verbiage in another.*

verbose *(ver-BOSE), adjective*
Wordy. That which uses unnecessary language is *verbose.*

> *This is not Hemingway's best work: long passages of the manuscript are strangely verbose and--let's face it-- downright boring.*

verdant *(VUR-dnt), adjective*
Green (with plant life). That which is lush with vegetation is *verdant.*

> *The verdant surroundings give one the feeling of being a million miles from the city, but from where we are standing now Nashville is only fifteen minutes away by car.*

veritable *(VER-ih-tuh-bull), adjective*
Authentic; true. That which is undeniably legitimate or actual is *veritable.*

> *The cardboard boxes contained a veritable treasure trove of Civil War artifacts, probably worth tens of thousands of dollars.*

vernacular *(ver-NAK-yoo-lur), noun and adjective*
The mode of expression in language accepted in a given circle. As an adjective, *vernacular* describes the quality of being common to a particular group's or region's speech.

> *I saw that Clement was once again intoxicated--or "blasted," to use the vernacular he seems to prefer.*

vertigo *(VUR-tih-go), noun*
A sensation of dizziness and disorientation. *Vertigo* is a feeling of tilting or spinning.

> *Jane was overcome with a sudden bout of vertigo as the ship left port.*

vestige *(VESS-tij), noun*
A remaining sample of something no longer common. That which represents something now lost is a *vestige*.

> *The last vestige of truly nomadic Indian life was wiped out at Wounded Knee; from that point on, Native Americans would be forced either to assimilate with the settlers or to live on the reservation.*

vexation *(vek-SAY-shun), noun*
Irritation. That which aggravates causes *vexation*.

> *"Where on earth is my horse?" Scarlett demanded in vexation.*

vicarious *(vi-KARE-ee-uss), adjective*
Arising from the experiences of others rather than one's own experience. To gain *vicarious* pleasure is to gain pleasure from actions not one's own.

> *I think Paul derives some vicarious thrill from making us fight; every spat we have seems to spring from something he's said to us.*

vindicate *(VIN-dih-kate), verb*
Proven correct or innocent despite previous indications to the contrary. To be *vindicated* is to have one's name cleared after being falsely suspected of something.

> *The test results vindicated the athlete: there was no trace of any illicit substance in his bloodstream.*

vindictive *(vin-DIK-tiv), adjective*
Mean-spirited; eager for revenge. A *vindictive* person is motivated by a desire for vengeance.

> *When angered, Lynn can be quite vindictive; those who work with her know that the most painless course is to stay on her good side.*

virile *(VIR-ul), adjective*
Forcefully masculine. Someone who is *virile* is characterized by the drive and energy thought to be common among men.

> *It was hard for me to picture my grandfather as the virile young man beaming out from that old photograph.*

visage *(VIZ-uj), noun*
The face. *Visage* can also mean "appearance."

> *It was a grim-visaged Roosevelt who addressed Congress the day after the Japanese attack.*

visceral *(VISS-er-ul), adjective*
Deeply felt. *Visceral* means "from the viscera," or bodily interior.

> *A visceral wave of panic ran through Clark's body as he listened to the air-raid siren blare.*

vitriolic *(vit-ree-OL-ik), adjective*
Acidic (literally, but also in tone). *Vitriolic* speech or writing is harsh and caustic.

> *McCarthy's vitriolic attacks on organizations with no actual Communist ties went completely unchallenged in the Senate.*

vivacious *(vy-VAY-shuss), adjective*
Spirited. That which is full of life is *vivacious*.

> *The novelist's characters are saucy and vivacious, but the situations they face are, alas, deadly dull.*

vociferous *(vo-SIF-er-uss), adjective*
Marked by noisy exclamation. That which demands attention with insistent loudness is *vociferous*.

Senator Billings objected vociferously to the amendment's inclusion in the bill.

volatile *(VOL-uh-tull), adjective*
Potentially unstable. That which is likely to shift or change suddenly is *volatile.*

We should have known that asking those two to work together after the divorce would lead to a volatile work environment.

voluptuous *(vuh-LUP-shoo-uss), adjective*
Sensually enjoyable. *Voluptuous* can also refer to that which calls to mind sensual pleasure.

The bestselling writer showed up fashionably late in a long black limousine, accompanied by a voluptuous companion whose name we never learned.

voracious *(vo-RAY-shuss), adjective*
Greedily hungry. Someone who is gluttonous or ravenous is *voracious.*

Tom is a voracious reader; I believe he has been through every volume in our public library.

wallow *(WALL-lo), verb*
To immerse oneself in utterly. Literally, to *wallow* in something is to roll around in it.

Joan's reviews were certainly unflattering, but in my opinion, she wallowed in self-pity after opening night and did the cast and crew of the show a disservice.

wanton *(WON-tun), adjective*
Completely unrestrained. *Wanton* can also mean "done without any justification."

Such wanton, pointless cruelty, even in the name of

science, is inexcusable.

watershed *(WAH-ter-shed), noun*
An important event that serves to distinguish two separate phases. Literally, a *watershed* is a ridge that diverts water in a new direction.

> *The new arms agreement is being touted as a watershed in East-West relations.*

wayfaring *(WAY-fare-ing), adjective*
Tending to travel by foot. A *wayfaring* person is one who walks as a means of conducting a journey.

> *My father, like many other men of his generation, spent some time as a wayfaring laborer during the depths of the Depression.*

wend *(wend), verb*
To go forward. To *wend* one's way is to proceed along a given course.

> *Hansel and Gretel, wending their way through the forest innocently, had no idea what awaited them at journey's end.*

writhe *(rythe), verb*
To twist (the body), especially in reaction to pain or strong sensation. To *writhe* is to twist the body or squirm.

> *The injured dog writhed in agony, but soon calmed down when the vet administered a local anesthetic.*

yahoo *(YA-hoo), noun*
A bumpkin. In Jonathan Swift's *Gulliver's Travels*, the *Yahoos* were a primitive, brutal race identical in form to humans.

> *I can't believe you appointed a yahoo like Ellis to such a sensitive post.*

yarmulke *(YAR-mul-kuh)*, *noun*

A skullcap-like headpiece worn by Jewish men (especially those following Orthodox or Conservative traditions). The *yarmulke* is worn during religious services or prayer.

> *Winston was unsure whether he was supposed to wear a yarmulke at the wedding; after all, he was a Gentile.*

yeshiva *(yuh-SHEE-vuh)*, *noun*

A school for Orthodox Jewish children. *Yeshiva* refers to two types of schools: one designed for children of elementary school age, and another for older students preparing for rabbinical life.

> *Paul is an old schoolmate; we went to yeshiva together.*

zealot *(ZEL-ut)*, *noun*

A fervent or fanatical partisan (in favor of a certain cause). A *zealot* is a person who shows great zeal.

> *Although he did not mind overlooking an occasional error in procedure, Mr. Fallow was a zealot when it came to posting correct numbers for an accounting period.*

zenith *(ZEE-nith)*, *noun*

The highest point attained. A *zenith* is the apex of something.

> *Koufax's career reached its zenith in 1963, when he won 25 games and was awarded the Cy Young Award unanimously.*

A Note on Pronunciation

Pronunciation keys given in this book are rendered phonetically; no special symbols or systems have been employed.

It should be noted that many of the words in this book have secondary and tertiary pronuciations--not listed here for the sake of simplicity--that are entirely correct. Furthermore, regional influences often affect the pronunciations of certain words. What has been offered is the most common accepted means of pronouncing a given word, but by no means the only way.